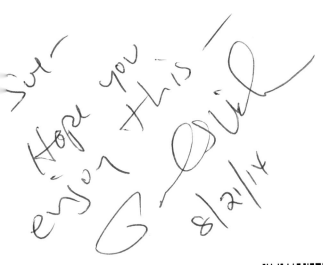

Sue—
Hope you
enjoy this

8/2/14

JACKSON

★ THE | GENERALS ★

JACKSON

The Iron-Willed Commander

★ THE | GENERALS ★

Paul S. Vickery, PhD

THOMAS NELSON
Since 1798

NASHVILLE   DALLAS   MEXICO CITY   RIO DE JANEIRO

Published in Nashville, Tennessee, by Thomas Nelson. Thomas Nelson is a registered trademark of Thomas Nelson, Inc.

Thomas Nelson, Inc., titles may be purchased in bulk for educational, business, fund-raising, or sales promotional use. For information, please e-mail SpecialMarkets@ ThomasNelson.com.

Library of Congress Cataloging-in-Publication Data

Vickery, Paul S.
  Jackson : the iron-willed commander / Paul S. Vickery.
  p. cm. -- (The generals)
  Includes bibliographical references and index.
  ISBN 978-1-59555-454-3 (hardback)
1. Jackson, Andrew, 1767-1845. 2. Generals--United States--Biography. 3. United States. Army--Biography. 4. Presidents--United States--Biography. 5. United States--Politics and government--1815-1861. I. Title.
  E382.V53 2012
  973.5'6092--dc23
  [B]
                          2011052619

Printed in the United States of America

12 13 14 15 16 WOR 6 5 4 3 2 1

Contents

A Note from the Editor

To contemplate the lives of America's generals is to behold both the best of us as a nation and the lesser angels of human nature, to bask in genius, and to be repulsed by arrogance and folly. It is these dichotomies that have defined the widely differing attitudes toward the "man on horseback," which have alternatively shaped the eras of our national memory. We have had our seasons of hagiography, in which our commanders can do no wrong and in which they are presented to the young, in particular, as unerring examples of nobility and manhood. We have had our revisionist seasons, in which all power corrupts—military power in particular—and in which the general is a reviled symbol of societal ills.

Fortunately, we have matured. We have left our adolescence

with its gushing extremes and have come to a more temperate view. Now, we are capable as a nation of celebrating Washington's gifts to us while admitting that he was not always a gifted tactician in the field. We can honor Patton's battlefield genius and decry the deformities of soul that diminished him. We can learn both from MacArthur at Inchon and from MacArthur at Wake Island.

We can also move beyond the mythologies of film and leaden textbook to know the vital humanity and the agonizing conflicts, to find a literary experience of war that puts the smell of boot leather and canvas in the nostrils and both the horror and the glory of battle in the heart. This will endear our nation's generals to us and help us learn the lessons they have to teach. Of this we are in desperate need, for they offer lessons of manhood in an age of androgyny, of courage in an age of terror of prescience in an age of myopia, and of self-mastery in an age of sloth. To know their story and their meaning, then, is the goal here and the hope that we will emerge from the experience a more learned, perhaps more gallant, and, certainly, more grateful people.

Stephen Mansfield

Series Editor, *The Generals*

Prologue

"The reign of King MOB seemed triumphant. I was glad to escape from the scene as soon as possible."

—Judge Story, John Quincy Adams supporter at
the inaugural ball

THE MORNING OF Wednesday, March 4, 1829, dawned sunny and bright in the nation's capital of Washington. Although patches of snow still lingered on the ground, it was a perfect day for a celebration. Not a room could be found as the city swelled by as much as thirty thousand spectators according to one account, many sleeping five to a bed. They had come from all over the nation to witness history in the making.[1] For today, the Tennessean Major General Andrew Jackson, the people's choice, was to be inaugurated the seventh president of the United States. It was to be an event unlike any previous inauguration because Jackson was a politician unlike any of his predecessors.

Born poor, he was a self-made man—one who represented the South and the western frontier and its expansionist interests. "Jackson and Reform" had been the campaign slogan, and change was about to happen. For the first time in our history, the president was not a member of the economic or social elite, and he did not come from the Eastern Seaboard state of either Massachusetts or Virginia. He was elected largely by voters who were not previously a part of the political process. All free white males now cast their ballots. Many were poor farmers on the rugged frontier, or mechanics (a term used to include all urban workers) and small businessmen. He was also the first and only president who carried in his body two bullets: one near his heart from a duel, and one in his shoulder from a shootout. He was indeed a change from the past.

Building on his reputation as a strong military leader, Superior Court judge, Indian fighter, representative of the common man as congressman and senator, and Washington outsider, General Jackson's victory symbolized a fundamental shift in both the conduct and the perception of the office of president. No longer would Eastern elites rule for their own regional and self-interest. With Jackson as the leader of the modern Democratic Party, no longer would the masses be underrepresented. The people now had a champion, a symbol, and they came out en masse to show their support.

"By ten o'clock the Avenue was crowded with carriages of every description," wrote one eyewitness and author, Margaret Bayard Smith, "from the splendid Barronet and coach, down to wagons and carts, filled with women and children, some in finery and some in rags for it was the peoples President and all would see him."[2] An early biographer of Jackson, James Parton, wrote, "It seemed as if half the nation had rushed at once into the Capital."[3] Suddenly "huzzas" filled the air as the general himself emerged from Gadsby's hotel to walk up to the Capitol.

Recognizing the importance of symbolism, he rejected a military procession in favor of one where he could mingle with his adoring supporters. He wore a simple black suit with a black tie covered by a long black overcoat. Impeded by the cheering crowd, the tall, erect, bare-headed Jackson and his entourage walked slowly down Pennsylvania Avenue. Jostling in the crowd for a better view, someone remarked, "There is the old man and his gray hair, there is the old veteran, there is Jackson."[4]

Entering the Capitol through the basement, he first attended the swearing in of Vice President John C. Calhoun in the Senate chambers. Jackson and Calhoun had won one of the bitterest campaigns in American history. Conspicuous by his absence, the outgoing John Quincy Adams had made known his intention not to be present at his successor's ceremony. Because Jackson believed Adams responsible for slander to his recently deceased wife, his beloved Rachel, the newly elected president was fine with this decision. Only polite yet frosty messages passed between the two. Adams, who would spend the day at the nearby home of a friend, sent Jackson a message stating he would vacate the White House and have it ready for occupancy on the fourth. Jackson sarcastically replied he hoped this didn't inconvenience his household staff. Finally it was time for the winner to take the oath of office.

"Thousands and thousands of people, without distinction of rank, collected in an immense mass round the Capitol," wrote Mrs. Smith, "silent, orderly and tranquil, with their eyes fixed on the front of that edifice[the Capitol], waiting for the appearance of the President on the portico."[5] "It is beautiful, it is sublime!" said Francis Scott Key, who had penned the song that was to become our national anthem.[6] At precisely noon to the sound of a military band and the discharge of cannon, Jackson appeared on a section of the east portico of the Capitol, a tradition continuing to this day. He bowed to the waiting crowd restrained only by a ship's cable stretched to the breaking point. At his appearance they erupted. "The shout that rent the air, still resounds in my ears," remembered Mrs. Smith.[7] Another observer wrote, "As if by miracle; all hats were off at once, and the dark tint which usually pervades a mixed map of men was turned, as if by magic, into the bright hue of ten thousand upturned and exultant human faces, radiant with sudden joy."[8] Soon the crowd quieted and awaited the inaugural address of their champion.

With his hands trembling, Jackson read his speech. Although he was capable of moving hardened military men with his rhetoric, this was not the time for motivation. In his ten-minute address, one of the briefest in history, President Jackson offered vague promises. He promised to reform Washington by "the correction of those abuses that have brought the patronage of the Federal Government into conflict with the freedom of elections," reform finances by "the extinguishment of the national debt," and balance the power of the federal government with states' rights, "taking care not to confound the powers they have reserved to themselves with those they have granted to the Confederacy [national government]." He closed with the words that he expected "a firm reliance on the goodness of the Power whose providence mercifully protected our national infancy, and has since upheld our liberties." His prayer was that "He will continue to make our beloved country the object of His divine care and gracious benediction."[9]

Although the crowd could not hear a word of what he said, they cheered lustily at its conclusion. Chief Justice John Marshall then administered the oath. After reciting the oath with a forceful voice while keeping his hand on the Bible, "the President took it [the Bible] from his hands, pressed his lips to it, laid it reverently down, then bowed again to the people—Yes, to the people in all their majesty." Again the spectators erupted.[10]

A mad rush ensued as the cable barrier was broken by the mass of humanity trying to touch their hero. With great difficulty Jackson made his way from the Capitol to Pennsylvania Avenue. Finally he mounted his horse and moved toward the Executive Mansion, followed by the human wave. "The living mass was impenetrable," wrote Mrs. Smith, "Country men, farmers, gentlemen, mounted and dismounted, boys, women and children, black and white. Carriages, wagons and carts all pursuing him to the President's house."[11] There the real celebration was about to take place. The "majesty" of the people was about to become the reign of "King MOB."

When Jackson and his entourage finally made their appearance at the White House, what a scene they found. "It was like the inundation of the northern barbarians into Rome,"[12] wrote Parton. The celebration is perhaps best described by those present. "The *Majesty of the People* had disappeared, and a rabble, a mob, of boys, negros, women, children, scrambling, fighting, romping. What a pity what a pity! No arrangements had been made, no police officers placed on duty and the whole house had been inundated by the rabble mob."[13] The crowd consisted not only of supporters and well-wishers, but also people seeking patronage from the new administration. "Here was the corpulent epicure grunting and sweating for breath, the dandy wishing he had no toes—the tight laced Miss, fearing her person might receive some permanently deforming impulse—the miser hunting for his pocketbook—the courtier looking for his watch—and the office seeker in an agony to reach the President."[14] The Executive Mansion, the White House, the president's residence, hitherto off limits except to a chosen few, had been converted into "the people's place," and they were going to make the most of their opportunity to celebrate.

"A profusion of refreshments had been provided. Orange punch by barrels full was made, but as the waiters opened the door to bring it out, a rush would be made," one writer observed, "the glasses broken, the pails of liquor upset, and the most painful confusion prevailed . . . wine and ice creams could not be brought out to the ladies, and tubs of punch were taken from the lower story into the garden, to lead the crowd from the rooms."[15] Jackson himself appeared to be in danger of injury by being pressed into the walls, so great was the number trying to squeeze into the rooms. Part of the solution was to get the exhausted

PROLOGUE ★ xv

president away from the confusion. With arms locked his aides pushed through the mob and took him back to Gadsby's. The remaining piece of the puzzle was to move the refreshments outside, knowing the thirsty would follow. It worked. Jackson was rescued, but the party continued.

"Cut glass and china to the amount of several thousand dollars had been broken in the struggle to get the refreshments, punch and other articles had been carried out in tubs and other buckets, but had it been in hogsheads it would have been insufficient, ice creams, and cakes, and lemonade for 20,000 people, for it is said that number were there, tho' I think the number exaggerated," detailed Mrs. Smith. "Ladies fainted, men were seen with bloody noses and such a scene of confusion took place as is impossible to describe,—those who got in could not get out by the door again, but had to scramble out of windows."[16] Mr. Gilmer, a representative from Georgia, was one who had to leave through an open window, "in doing which, I had to sustain with a weak leg from a fracture scarcely healed the weight of Mrs. Floyd equaling three hundred pounds."[17]

"On such an occasion it was difficult to keep anything like order, but it was mortifying to see men, with boots heavy with mud, standing on the damask satin covered chairs, from their eagerness to get a sight of the President."[18] Another observer was even more specific: "One hundred-and-fifty dollar official chairs [were] profaned by the feet of clod-hoppers."[19] Perhaps Judge Story, a great supporter of Adams and critic of Jackson, summarized the opposition feelings: "I never saw such a mixture. The reign of King MOB seemed triumphant. I was glad to escape from the scene as soon as possible."[20] Few truly realized the fundamental shift in American politics that took place with this inauguration.

Although the total value of the destruction was no more than a few thousand dollars, the image of the change in Washington cannot be overstated. Gone were the days when the president was remote from the average person—aloof from the rough-and-tumble of day-to-day politics—and representative of the elite. Now the president was expected to rub shoulders with all social classes. Also past was the custom of only well-dressed elites coming to the presidential levees. Buckskins and homespun were now common sights. Jackson was the very personification of the average citizen, the one who worked for a living, unafraid to get his hands dirty, and a symbol of the "majesty" of the common man.

At the opening of the nineteenth century, America was changing. As the population grew and moved west, the center of political power moved with it. The powerful wealthy traders and large landholders of the Eastern Seaboard states, who had dominated and ruled the country since its beginning, now had to reckon with the growing number of frontiersmen and smaller landholders whose interests were different and often at odds with theirs. They demanded land and access to markets. It mattered little if those lands belonged to native peoples or to nations across the seas. Fortune favored those who took what they wanted and were prepared to fight to maintain it. Support went to those who promised to open these lands to settlement and access to water transportation routes for trade. The stage was set for a hero, a "man of the people," to emerge and represent this new, more democratic spirit. Onto this stage came the man who would give voice to their aspirations and would himself be a product of the opportunities available for a man who knew what he wanted and was prepared to take it whatever the cost.

How a poor southern boy, orphaned at fifteen, with seemingly no other credentials than a contentious iron will, a desire to improve his situation in life, and a belief in the power and greatness of the American citizen, arose to become president is the topic of this work. Its purpose is to demonstrate that the leadership qualities developed by Jackson as he rose in station by hard work, a firm belief in his abilities, faith in God, sheer force of will, help from others, and perhaps a bit of luck propelled him from an obscure rural village to the epitome of public office, ushered in what one author labeled "The Age of Jackson," and fundamentally changed the paradigm of how Americans selected their leaders.

The second president to emerge as a national hero through his military successes, he would certainly not be the last. Jackson, however, had none of the social or financial advantages inherited by our first military hero made president, George Washington. Traditionally military rank was determined by birth, wealth, or social standing. Like Washington, however, Jackson learned, developed, and honed his skills as he grew and rose through the military command structure. With victories over both Indians and powerful European nations, he proved his abilities as a military tactician and leader of men. He therefore demonstrated that leadership and respect can and must be earned through trial and that America was the place where this could take place.

Where possible in this work, the characters are allowed to speak for themselves, especially in regard to their religious beliefs, attitudes, descriptions, and feelings. Thus readers may interpret individual motives that at times, like our own, may appear contradictory. We can also view how the individual's and the nation's perspectives changed over time. Although always controversial, Jackson was the most popular and beloved man in America in his time. Love him or hate him—and there are still those on both sides—he is one of the most colorful and successful of our military leaders who used this experience to arise to the highest office in the land.[21]

CHAPTER ONE

A Boy Becomes a Man

"I could throw him three times out of four, but he would never *stay throwed*. . . . [Jackson] never *would* give up."
—A childhood friend

THE EARLY LIFE of Andrew Jackson was marked by sorrow, hardship, and poverty. Like many of his contemporaries, he was forced to grow up fast, work hard, and take responsibility far beyond his years. The son of a hardscrabble farmer in the late eighteenth century did not expect an easy life, especially when his father died before that child was even born. A Jackson intimate, Francis Parton Blair, believed, "Jackson owed less to birthright and more to self-help than any other great man, not only in our history but in any other."[1] His mother, his extended family, and the Presbyterian Church, including the school that met there in the meetinghouse, played a great role in his formative years.

Like thousands of other immigrants settling in the Appalachian region of the American colonies, Andrew Jackson Sr., the impoverished father of the future hero of New Orleans, arrived in 1765 from northern Ireland. With him came his wife, Elizabeth Hutchinson, described as a "stout woman" and "a poor man's daughter," along with their two sons Hugh and Robert.[2] Almost immediately they traveled to the Waxhaw settlement, roughly 160 miles northwest of Charles Town (The name was officially changed to Charleston in August, 1783. The British had departed the city in December, 1782.), South Carolina. The Jacksons chose this area because several of Elizabeth's sisters as well as other Irish Protestant families, mainly Presbyterian, had settled this area in 1751.

Located between the Waxhaw and Cane Creeks, it was the former home of the Waxhaw tribe, hence the name, but now consisted of only a few peaceful Catawbas. An area filled with pine trees, hardwoods, and packed red clay, it required effort to coax a living from the ground. Jackson settled on a two-hundred-acre plot of land near Twelve Mile Creek. Whether he actually owned this land, however, is disputed. James Parton, who researched the issue, believed "that Andrew Jackson, the elder, never owned one acre of land in America."[3] After two years of backbreaking labor, Andrew Jackson Sr. died of unknown causes, leaving two small sons, a pregnant wife, and precious little else.[4]

There is an often-told tale that neighbors fended off their grief for the loss of their friend during his wake by imbibing a bit too much of the local brew. The day following the wake his friends placed the coffin on a sled pulled by a mule. The trip to the grave site, through ice, snow, and broken limbs, was thirsty work. The mourners paused several times to refresh themselves as they had brought "liquor along & would stop at the branches . . . & take a drink."[5] Thus when the party arrived at the grave site, in the twilight they realized that the sled no longer bore the coffin. Somehow it slipped off, unnoticed, undoubtedly because of the grief shared by the pallbearers, as they mounted a steep creek bank. The interment took place later than expected that evening.

Only weeks later, the widow gave birth. She named the child Andrew Jackson after her late husband. Exactly where Jackson was born has been the subject of some debate since the exact border between the two states was not finalized until 1772. Parton claimed, "It was in a small log house, in the province of North Carolina, less than a quarter of a mile from the boundary line between North and South Carolina, that the birth took place."[6] Robert Remini wrote, "Following the interment [of Jackson Sr.], Elizabeth went to the home of her sister, Jane Crawford, and there on March 15, 1767, in the Lancaster District, South Carolina, she gave birth."[7] In any case the family remained in the Crawford household because "Mrs. Crawford was an invalid, and Mrs. Jackson was permanently established in the family as housekeeper and poor relation."[8] Thus Andrew grew up a South Carolinian. It was there, among the pines and red clay, that young Andrew spent the formative first twelve or so years of his life. From his rural roots, we get a glimpse of how his education, environment, and above all his mother influenced the man. A look at his spirited youthful habits and near juvenile delinquency tendencies should give hope to all young people and their parents: if Jackson can turn out all right, despite his youthful indiscretions, so can anyone![9]

Because his mother wanted Andrew to become a Presbyterian minister, she took him weekly to services at the Waxhaw Presbyterian meetinghouse. In the rural South, a meetinghouse was more than a church. Many served as schools during the week and were the social centers of communities. There Jackson "probably spent between three and four hours nearly every Sunday for about fourteen years hearing prayers, psalms, scripture, sermons and hymns."[10] Thus biblical terms and stories filled his mind, animated his thoughts, and were formative in his developing worldview. He probably learned more from hearing than reading, as he would later become a much better speaker than writer. Throughout his life, Jackson, who stated he read three chapters of Scripture daily, used biblical allusions and even compared his life's struggles with those of King David. He also memorized the Westminster Shorter Catechism, which provided him with both scriptural and theological training.[11]

Initially young Andrew attended a school typical for his area. It was a low-roofed log cabin, fourteen by twenty feet, erected by the community and capable of holding perhaps twenty to twenty-five students. A fireplace took up almost one entire side.[12] The scene would have been the same across the South: "An itinerant schoolmaster presents himself in a neighborhood; the responsible farmers pledge him a certain number of pupils," and the school was established for the season.[13] In this one-room schoolhouse Jackson began his education. "Among a crowd of urchins, seated on the slab benches . . . fancy a tall, slender boy, with blue bright eyes, a freckled face, an abundance of long sandy hair . . . with bare feet dangling and kicking—and you have in your mind's eye a picture of Andy."[14] He eventually grew to be at least six feet tall, very lean, "even cadaverous," with very thin arms and legs, and never weighed more than 145 pounds. Despite his unimposing physique, his intense bright blue eyes, when aimed at someone, "had a powerful effect. . . . They riveted attention; they commanded obedience; and they could terrorize."[15]

Soon, however, his mother placed him in a more rigorous academy, taught by Dr. William Humphries, that met in the Presbyterian meetinghouse. There he received the rudiments of reading and writing and learned to "cast accounts." Another early biographer and Jackson friend, John Eaton, added, "Here he was placed on the study of the dead languages [probably Greek and Latin] and continued until the revolutionary war."[16] Somehow his mother found the money to also send him to study with the Presbyterian minister James White Stephenson. Although Andrew was not an avid reader, his tastes led to stories of military actions and strong heroes. Much as his biblical hero was King David, his secular hero became William Wallace, the Scottish hero of their war for independence from England (1296–1305). Published in 1809, Jane Porter's book *Scottish Chiefs* became a favorite of his, and he sought to emulate the traits displayed by Wallace.

The results of his formal education were not impressive even by the standards of the day. "He was never a well-informed man. He was never addicted to books. He never learned to write the English language correctly. . . . He never learned to spell correctly." At times he spelled the same word two or three different ways, even in the same letter.[17] In fact, his lack of education became a personal and political issue exploited by his enemies as he advanced in public office. For example, in 1833, Harvard University awarded President Jackson an honorary degree. A Harvard graduate, President John Quincy Adams, whom Jackson had previously defeated for reelection in a very bitter personal campaign, refused to participate. He wrote to the president of the university, "As myself an affectionate child of our Alma Mater, I would not be present to witness her disgrace in conferring her highest literary honors upon a barbarian who could not write a sentence of grammar and hardly could spell his own name."[18]

If his literary education was lacking, his knowledge of human nature and his physical development were not. Vignettes from his childhood depict a willful boy with a chip on his shoulder, a boy who used his physical abilities and strength of will to overcome life's obstacles. "Andy was a wild, frolicsome, willful, mischievous, daring, reckless boy; generous to a friend but never content to submit to a stronger enemy. He was passionately fond of those sports which are mimic battles," wrote Parton.[19] A former schoolmate said of him, "I could throw him three times out of four, but he would never *stay throwed*. . . . [He] never *would* give up."[20] This tenacious quality served him well in future years.

Further insight into Jackson's formative years and the character of his mother is provided by Parton. In an interview with a ninety-two-year-old slave woman, known as Aunt Phyllis, who personally knew Jackson, she recollected that "he was the most mischievous of all the youngsters thereabouts; always up to some prank and getting into trouble." She recalled Mrs. Jackson as "a stout woman who was always knitting or spinning; 'a very good woman, and very much respected.'"[21]

Even as a youth, Jackson felt the need to be taken seriously and to assert his personality. Constantly on the defensive, perhaps in an effort to prove himself or fulfill some hole left by not having a father, Jackson was a friend and protector to those who agreed with him and submitted to his authoritarian nature. However, "his equals and superiors found him self-willed, somewhat overbearing, easily offended, *very* irascible, and, upon the whole 'difficult to get along with.'"[22] Not only could Andy hold his own in a physical confrontation, but his swearing abilities were also becoming legendary.

He apparently learned to swear at a very early age. "He needed to begin early," opined Parton, "in order to acquire that wonderful mastery of the art to which he attained in after life, surpassing all known men in the fluency and chain-shot force and complication of his oaths."[23] Even his pious mother was unable to curb his tongue. It was not until the death of his beloved Rachel, and obviously in her honor, that he ceased his coarse language. "Except on occasions of extreme excitement, few and far between," wrote Parton, "he never again used . . . 'profane language;' not even the familiar phrase 'By the Eternal.'"[24]

With the reading of the Declaration of Independence in Philadelphia on July 4, 1776, the American colonies formally broke from their colonial masters. A legend, spurious according to biographer Hendrik Booraem but still widely told, involves how Jackson's community heard the news. A Philadelphia newspaper with a synopsis of this document reached the Waxhaws in August 1776. The monthly arrival of news from what would become the nation's capital was always a big event for the settlers. Because of the high illiteracy rate, a "public reader" was selected to share the contents with an eager audience. Nine-year-old Andrew received the honor. According to his own words, at that time he possessed "a shrill penetrating voice." Perhaps more important for the hearers, he "could read a paper clear through without getting hoarse," and he "could read right off, without stopping to spell out the words."[25]

Thus did news of the rebellion reach the Carolinas, an area consisting largely of supporters of the newly formed government, known as Whigs, yet also possessing a sizable Tory, or loyalist, population. In 1779, the war came in earnest to the South. Both Whigs and loyalists took up arms supporting their respective sides. Even within families loyalties could be divided. The war had a devastating effect on the Jackson family and forever changed young Andrew. Hugh was the first to die, as the fighting became vicious, personal, and bloody.

In the spring of 1779, Andrew's oldest brother, sixteen-year-old Hugh, left home to fight with Colonel William Davie's regiment. At the Battle of Stono Ferry, on a hot June day, although racked by fever and excused from fighting, Hugh joined the battle and perished soon after from "excessive heat of the weather, and fatigues of the day."[26] Although grieving the loss of her son, Elizabeth supported her two remaining sons, Robert and Andrew, in attending local militia drills. There thirteen-year-old Andrew learned a lesson he would never forget—the value of good training and sound discipline.

The spring of 1780 saw the fall of Charles Town, South Carolina, to Sir Henry Clinton. Lieutenant Colonel Banastre Tarleton and his green-clad British Legion then moved west, wreaking havoc into the Waxhaws. Soon his name would become anathema to the rebels, and he would earn the nickname "Bloody Tarleton." On May 29, his mounted troops surprised Colonel Abraham Buford's Virginia regiment in an open field. To the sound of a blaring British bugle, Tarleton's cavalry attacked Buford's vulnerable rear guard.

Seeing his men cut down by the onrushing British, Buford ordered a white flag raised and his men to ground their arms as a sign of surrender. Asking for quarter, he expected to receive the treatment awarded to any civilized prisoners of war. He miscalculated. "Not a man was spared," wrote Dr. Robert Brownfield, ". . . for fifteen minutes after every man was prostrate, they [the British] went over the ground, plunging their bayonets into everyone that exhibited any signs of life."[27] One hundred thirteen were slaughtered, and another one hundred fifty left for dead. These men were brought to the Waxhaw Church, where Andrew, Robert, and their mother cared for them. The battle was quickly called a massacre, and the term *Tarleton's quarter* entered the American lexicon.

In July 1780, thirteen-year-old Andrew Jackson and his sixteen-year-old brother joined Major William Davie's dragoons.

Jackson recalled he was quickly appointed as a "mounted orderly or messenger, for which I was well fitted, being a good rider and knowing all the roads." Davie also presented him with a pistol and made such an impression on the young man that "to the end of Andrew Jackson's life his absolute ideal of an officer and gentleman" was Major Davie.[28] Only weeks after joining, Jackson experienced his first action at the Battle of Hanging Rock. Although it was declared an American victory, the results could have been more successful if the troops had not discovered and emptied the British rum store.

The Jackson boys smelled powder again in April 1781. A British party had come to the Waxhaws to search out and destroy Whig resistance. About forty of the local militia formed up at the meetinghouse to confront them. The ensuing confrontation forced the rebels from the building. Robert and Andrew spent the night hiding in a thicket. The next day, seeking food, they went to the house of their cousin Lieutenant Thomas Crawford. Through a tip from a Tory sympathizer, the house was surrounded, and the boys were captured. "The dragoons . . . began to destroy, with wild riot and noise the contents of the house. Crockery, glass, and furniture were dashed to pieces; beds emptied, the clothing of the family torn to rags; even the clothes of the infant Mrs. Crawford carried in her arms were not spared."[29] The brutality of warfare left both emotional and physical scars on young Andrew.

During the melee, a British officer ordered Jackson to clean his boots. With firmness, yet in a respectful tone, he answered, "Sir, I am a prisoner of war, and claim to be treated as such."[30]

With glaring eyes and "like a wild beast" the officer swung at Andrew with his sword. Instinctively the boy raised his left hand in protection. The bloody result was a gash on both his hand and his head. He carried these scars to his grave. The officer then ordered Robert to clean his boots. He, too, demurred and was given a blow that knocked him senseless.[31] Both boys, along with about twenty other prisoners, were then force-marched to Camden about forty miles away.

"When we were taken prisoners we were thrown into jail in Camden with about 250 others," remembered Jackson. "No attention whatever was paid to the wounds or to the comfort of the prisoners, and the smallpox having broken out among them . . . many fell victims to it. . . . I also had become infected with the contagion."[32] Both boys were rescued by their mother as she contrived to get them included in a prisoner exchange. The three of them possessed only two horses. Because Robert was weakened "by a severe bowel complaint and the wound he had received on his head," he suffered even more than the ailing Andrew, so he and Elizabeth rode. Having lost his shoes and jacket to the British, Andrew trudged the forty-five miles home barefoot. Two days later Robert died, and Andrew was still clinging to life, suffering from the dreaded smallpox.

After several months of nursing Andrew back to some semblance of health, Elizabeth left for Charles Town. Two of her nephews were sick in a British prison ship, and she wanted to "minister to the comfort" of them. Her "mother's advice" in her last words to her son was to make friends by being honest and keep them by continuing steadfast: "Andy . . . never tell a lie, nor take what is not your own, nor sue . . . for slander. . . . Settle them cases yourself."[33] In the summer of 1781, while nursing sick prisoners, she contracted cholera and died. She was buried in an unmarked grave outside the city. Her possessions, "a sorry bundle," were sent back to "her sorrowing son at Waxhaw."[34] The effect of the loss of his mother was deep and lasting. "I felt utterly alone," he lamented, "and tried to recall her last words to me."[35] Many times throughout his life he sought to find her remains and bring them back to the old church cemetery at Waxhaw. There he intended to build a monument to both parents. There are no markers for any of his immediate family, however.

As the American Revolution ended, Andrew Jackson, not yet fifteen years of age, was alone in the world—an orphan without siblings. The experiences of his formative years greatly influenced future decisions both as a battlefield commander and as president. They taught him he could withstand physical pain, illness, and grief; and with an iron will, persistence, and courage, he could overcome them all. He had witnessed firsthand the brutality and often senseless cruelty of warfare; he recognized the need for sacrifice in the cause for freedom. In the future, he would not balk at requiring sacrifice, either of himself or others, to further those objectives he considered essential. The chip, evident on his shoulder from an early age, grew even larger. Never would he forget how the British had caused him and his country great suffering. Soon—very soon—they would pay for that.

CHAPTER TWO

A Lawyer Is Born

"As a person of unblemished moral character . . . [who] appears to possess a competent degree of knowledge in the Law [Jackson could] plead and practice as an Attorney."

—Judges Samuel Ashe and John Williams signing
Jackson's law license

ON OCTOBER 19, 1781, the British forces under Lord Cornwallis surrendered at Yorktown, Virginia. Nearly two years later, on September 3, 1783, the Treaty of Paris made it official. The former colonies were no longer under British authority. Independence came at last to the fledgling nation. What would the young, wounded, and alone Andrew Jackson now do?

At some point after Yorktown, Jackson moved in with an uncle, Major Thomas Crawford. Writing years later and admittedly forgetting what the argument was all about, Jackson described a confrontation with another boarder at the Crawfords, Captain Galbraith an American commissary. When Galbraith, whom Jackson described as "being of a very proud and haughty disposition," threatened to physically chastise him, Jackson replied that he "had arrived at the age to know my rights, and although weak and feeble from disease, I had the courage to defend them, and if he attempted anything of that kind I would most assuredly send him to the other world." Galbraith backed off, but Crawford decided Andrew needed to move elsewhere.[1] He moved to the home of Joseph White, the uncle of Mrs. Crawford, and for about six months he worked in his saddler's shop.[2]

During the time the British occupied Charles Town, several socially prominent and wealthy Whigs fled to the Waxhaws as virtual refugees. There several of the young men befriended Andrew and cultivated in him their love of "the frolicsome spirit of the youth." What little money he had was soon squandered as "he ran races and rode races, gambled a little, drank a little, fought cocks occasionally, and comported himself in the style usually affected by dissipated young fools of that day."[3] With the British evacuation of Charles Town in December 1782, these families returned to their homes, and Jackson followed.

It was there that Jackson developed his taste for fine clothes, gaming, and above all, fine racehorses. Throughout his life, the tall, lean Jackson cut an impressive figure by his dress and deportment apparently learned as a young man in the sophisticated society of Charleston. An early biographer, Henry Lee, wrote, "There can be little doubt that at this period he imbibed that high sense of honour, and unstudied elegance of air for which he has since been distinguished."[4] Soon, however, his gambling debts and high living drove him back home where for a period he continued his studies and even acted as schoolmaster near the Waxhaw Methodist Episcopal Church.[5]

Restlessness and a strong desire to improve his standing both financially and socially, coupled with the formalization of the treaty ending the Revolution, motivated the seventeen-year-old to seek a new start. He chose to "read" (that is, study) law, and he selected Salisbury, North Carolina, as the place to begin his new life. For a poor, landless individual like Jackson, law was one way to acquire wealth as well as social standing. Many clients, having little cash, would pay with crops, animals, or property deeds. To pass the bar examination, most southern attorneys apprenticed themselves to practicing lawyers and thereby learned the trade by reading the law, copying legal documents, listening to cases, as well as being general errand boys for the tutors. Thus in 1784, Jackson apprenticed himself to an eminent lawyer, Spruce McCay, and made his way the nearly seventy-five miles north to Salisbury, the county seat of Rowan County. There he joined fellow students, including a future important connection, John McNairy, in quarters above the Rowan House tavern.

For the next two years Jackson read law. His reputation in Salisbury, however, was not based primarily on his legal pursuits. He was better known for his social activities. "Andrew Jackson was the most roaring, rollicking, game-cocking, horse-racing, card-playing, mischievous fellow that ever lived in Salisbury," recalled one resident of the town. Others described him as "more in the stable than in the office," and the "head of all the rowdies hereabouts." Another believed, "He did not trouble the law-books much."[6]

Undoubtedly one of the most well-known stories about Jackson arising from his life in Salisbury involved his bringing two prostitutes to a Christmas ball. Salisbury had a dancing school, and the dapper Andrew attended. Asked to manage the annual ball and thinking it a great joke, he invited mother and daughter, Molly and Rachel Wood, "two women of ill repute." Not realizing it was a joke, they arrived decked out in their finest. No one laughed. The Woods were soon asked to leave. Upon hearing that Andrew was responsible for this incident, the proper ladies let him have it. Humbly, he apologized and asked forgiveness, and perhaps because of his charm, he was quickly absolved.[7]

Another well-publicized event involved not only Andrew but also McNairy and Jackson's cousin and fellow student Will Crawford. They and several of their cronies celebrated an event in the tavern. About midnight, well into their cups, it was decided that the wine glasses and decanters used by the revelers "ought never to be profaned to any baser use." Thus they were smashed. Well, what about the table? It, too, was part of the hilarious evening and would also be "profaned" by future use. In short order it was turned into splinters. Next they destroyed the chairs, the bed, and every other article of furniture in the room, and they ended by shredding the bed clothes and curtains. Finally all that could burn was thrown into the fire.[8]

The significance of these events is not that they

happened—such happenings were not all that uncommon in a culture that celebrated both the good and the bad times of life by consuming copious quantities of alcohol—but that they failed to have a negative effect on Jackson's reputation. His pranks were viewed as harmless and good-spirited. When Jackson later ran for president, an elderly woman remembered him as being such a "rake" that she did not permit her husband to bring him into the house, but they were allowed to drink and discuss horse racing in the barn. With that she had no quarrel. Concerning his bid for the presidency, she remarked, "What! Jackson up for President? *Jackson*? *Andrew* Jackson? The Jackson that used to live in Salisbury? . . . Well, if Andrew Jackson can be President, anybody can."[9]

In 1787, Jackson finished his law studies under the tutelage of Colonel John Stokes, a former Revolutionary War hero and well-respected attorney. He had lost a hand in the war and was known for using the silver-knobbed prosthetic to emphasize his point by banging it resoundingly on the table. After only six months with Stokes, Jackson appeared before a board of two judges of the North Carolina Superior Court of Law and Equity for his examination. On September 26, he received his law license. Because he was "sufficiently recommended to us as a person of unblemished moral character, and upon examination had before us, appears to possess a competent degree of knowledge in the Law," he was able ". . . to plead and practice as an Attorney." Both judges, Samuel Ashe and John Williams, signed the license.[10]

A few months later he received an offer from his fellow

carouser and law student, John McNairy, who had been appointed
Superior Court judge over the western district of North
Carolina. This area, present-day Tennessee, extended from
the Appalachians to the Mississippi River. McNairy appointed
Jackson as public prosecutor. He also appointed another of their
cronies, Thomas Searcy, as court clerk. They and several other
young lawyers made plans to rendezvous at Morganton, North
Carolina, to cross the mountains to Jonesboro, the principal
town in East Tennessee.[11]

In April, 1778, Jackson arrived in Jonesboro, and according to three eyewitnesses, he was "riding one horse and leading
another; that the horse he was riding was a race horse; that he
had a pair of holsters buckled across the front of his saddle," and
on the other horse were a shotgun, a pack, and bulging saddle-
bags. Following Jackson was "a goodly pack of fox hounds."[12] He
and the others would wait until fall to make their final push the
183-mile journey through hostile Cherokee country to Nashville.
In Jonesboro, Jackson acquired his first slave—"a Negro woman
named Nancy about eighteen or twenty years of age." She would
not be his last.[13] It was here also, while defending a client in an
otherwise unremarkable case, that Jackson fought his first duel.

Colonel Waightstill Avery, a well-respected attorney and
one with whom Jackson considered apprenticing because of his
extensive library, was serving as prosecuting attorney for the
state. During the course of the trial, which was not going well for
the defense, Avery sarcastically made fun of a legal position taken
by Jackson. Enraged, Jackson took his pen and quickly wrote out
a challenge, immediately delivering it to the startled Avery. "My

charecter you have Injured; and further you have Insulted me in the presence of a court and larg audianc," read the note. "I therefore call upon you as a gentleman to give me Satisfaction for the Same; and . . . to give me an nswer immediately without Equivocation."[14] The arrangements made, the two met just after sundown. After measuring the ground and toeing the line, the two fired into the air. They shook hands and remained friends thereafter. Neither was injured, but honor, so important in the South, was maintained.[15]

During his six months in Jonesboro, Jackson demonstrated he was not a man to be trifled with. Having obtained a slave, he was on the way to acquiring the trappings of a gentleman. He defended what he perceived as an affront to his honor. Particularly in the South, a man without honor was not taken seriously. His immediate actions, both in writing the challenge to Avery and taking charge during a fire that nearly destroyed Jonesboro, indicate he was capable of acting quickly.[16] In a crisis others recognized his innate leadership and followed him. The boy who would not "stay throwed" or polish British boots was becoming a man who would be taken seriously and be respected—and woe to the man who did not do so. In late September, with about sixty families and an armed escort, he left for Nashville.

The journey through that part of Tennessee was dangerous. Native Americans resisted the ever-growing number of settlers encroaching on their hunting grounds, and attacks on travelers were common. One night, after traveling thirty-six hours—two days and a night—with only minimal rest, the roughly one hundred persons traveling with Jackson made camp. Supposedly they had passed through the most dangerous area. Leaning against a tree, smoking his pipe, Jackson was dozing when he noted the hooting of owls. It appeared they were calling to one another. Instinctively Jackson became wide awake and wakened his friend Searcy. "There are Indians all around us," whispered Jackson. "I have heard them in every direction. They mean to attack before daybreak."[17] Quietly, he roused the rest of the camp, and they continued their journey unharmed. Unfortunately a white hunting party happened on the spot and fell asleep by the burning fires. Before dawn, the Indians attacked, killing all but one hunter. In this, his first encounter with hostile Indians, it was again Jackson who recognized the danger, took command, and hustled the settlers off to safety. He was quickly developing a reputation as a leader.

CHAPTER THREE

Rachel and Nashville

She was "the best story-teller, the best dancer, the sprightliest companion, the most dashing horsewoman in the country."

—An early description of Rachel

THE SETTLEMENT THAT greeted Jackson and his group when they arrived on October 26, 1788, was only eight years old. Founded in a fertile valley on a bend of the Cumberland River and surrounded by hardwoods, Nashville consisted of a distillery, a couple of taverns, a courthouse, two stores, and an odd assortment of bark tents, cabins, and horse sheds. The Indians, unwilling to give up such a fertile area with abundant game, were a constant threat. Settlers went nowhere without being armed. They heartily welcomed the newcomers and the protection that more arms provided. His first impressions are not recorded, so we do not know what twenty-one-year-old Jackson thought when he arrived at the place where he would find his home, his future, and his true love.

Among the original settlers of this community were John Donelson, a surveyor and land speculator, his wife, Rachel, and their eleven children. The youngest was the beautiful Rachel, born in 1767, the same year as Andrew. In December 1779, Donelson led a party of 40 men and 120 women and children on a nearly 980-mile unexplored voyage "down the Holston [River], down the Tennessee to its junction with the Ohio, then up the Ohio, and up the Cumberland to French Salt Spring [Nashville]."[1] The four-month voyage, chronicled in a diary by Donelson, was an incredible adventure including the birth of a baby, near starvation, frostbite, and constant Indian attacks. One boat, containing a family quarantined by smallpox, was forced to float at a distance from the others. Hostile Cherokees unwittingly captured the unfortunate party and quickly put them to death. The pox, however, spread and nearly decimated the entire tribe.

"Procured some buffalo meat: though poor it was palatable," recorded Donelson on March 26. The next day, he "killed a swan, which was very delicious."[2] Twice the party was nearly swept away by strong currents as they passed through "The Swirl" and "Muscle Shoals," but "by the hand of Providence we are now preserved from this danger."[3] Finally on April 24, 1780, the exhausted and hungry remaining members of the party arrived at Nashville.

In 1785, due to a severe corn shortage in the settlement, the

Donelson clan moved to Kentucky (then still a part of Virginia). There, at the age of seventeen, Rachel married Lewis Robards. After the food crisis diminished, Donelson and his family returned to Nashville, leaving Rachel and her husband behind. While surveying the wilderness, Donelson was murdered, and his wallet was stolen. We do not know whether he was ambushed by Indians or a white settler. Rachel believed Indians could not have killed her father because he "knew their ways too well to be caught by them."[4]

The marriage between Rachel and Lewis was an unhappy one. The former Revolutionary War captain was jealous and suspicious of any man who spoke with her, while at the same time he reportedly betrayed her with other women. Contemporaries described him as "educated, handsome, polished in manners of conversation, and possessed of those attributes supposed to attract women." Yet "all accounts are unanimous in representing him as high tempered and jealous." Thus although possessing admirable qualities, he "could not get along with any woman very long at a time."[5] Rachel possessed qualities that made her attractive to men. She was "the best story-teller, the best dancer, the sprightliest companion, the most dashing horsewoman in the country."[6] She was also described as "of the brunette type, not very tall and well built." In addition, she was "mentally keen and bright, naturally cheerful and witty . . . had a talent as a musician, could sing and was very companionable among friends."[7] When Lewis Robards found Rachel speaking with a boarder in his mother's house in a manner he found suspicious, he ordered her to return to her mother's house along the Cumberland. Her brother Samuel traveled to Kentucky and brought her home to the widowed Mrs. Donelson's blockhouse.

Soon, however, Robards regretted his decision and begged Rachel to take him back. The fact that she agreed was probably due to the fact that her prospects as a divorcee on the frontier were worse than being in an unhappy relationship. Divorces were hard to come by and expensive, and the process could take years. She therefore consented, and Robards joined his wife. Although Lewis had purchased land, he moved in with Rachel and her mother because he feared Indian attacks. Boarders, especially men who could wield a weapon, were welcomed on the frontier. Into this tense marital relation arrived "the most roaring, rollicking, game-cocking, horse-racing, card-playing, mischievous fellow that ever lived" to board at the Donelson house. Jackson could not help being attracted to Rachel. The situation was a tinderbox awaiting only a spark.

The love affair that arose between the vivacious, flirtatious Rachel and the impetuous, fiercely competitive Andrew would alter the course of both lives. Apparently it was practically love at first sight and became a love that only deepened and grew stronger over the years. Jackson became so devoted to her that he fought duels to defend her honor. After their marriage he would write to her at every opportunity to calm her fears for his safety and well-being. For example, "I have this moment recd, your letter," he wrote to her, ". . . and what sincere regret it gives me on the one hand to view your distress of mind and what real pleasure it would afford me on the other to return to your arms." In the same letter he assured her, "I have wrote you every post since I left you—and will continue to do so."[8] On the other hand, Rachel risked the slander and gossip that came from involving herself with another man while still married to Robards. In Jackson she found the love, acceptance, and protection not provided by her jealous first husband. Her relationship with Jackson became one of mutual respect, love, and dependence.

Arriving about the same time in Nashville was John Overton, a future judge and Jackson friend who had previously been a boarder with Lewis Robards's mother in Kentucky and understood the tension between the couple. In fact Overton was instrumental in reconciling the two. He and Jackson took up boarding in a small cabin near the main blockhouse where they shared the same bed. Thus two available handsome men lived in close proximity to Rachel. It did not take long for the jealous husband to suspect Jackson of mischief.

One afternoon, a party of women, protected as always by an armed guard, went out to pick blackberries. Robards also went. At some point Robards said to several of the guards he believed Jackson "was too intimate with his wife." Someone soon informed Jackson of this statement. Immediately he confronted Robards, informing him that "if he ever connected his name with that of Mrs. Robards in that way again, he would cut his ears out of his head." Furthermore, the outraged Jackson stated that "he was tempted to do it any how."[9] Robards immediately set out to obtain a warrant against Jackson. A guard was dispatched from the blockhouse to serve the summons and accompany the charged man back to the court. Robards accompanied him. Along the way the prisoner asked one guard if he could use his butcher knife. Jackson was well liked, and after assuring the guard he would harm no one, Jackson was given the knife. Examining the point and running his hands over the sharp edge, Jackson eyed Robards. The intent was unmistakable, and Robards fled. He failed to appear at court, and the charges were dismissed.[10]

Overton suggested that "the unpleasant situation of living in a family where there was so much disturbance" was not helping either him or Jackson and therefore they should find other accommodations further away. Jackson agreed, but mindful of his reputation and honor, he did not want to leave under a shadow of doubt. He again confronted Robards. Recalling what Mrs. Donelson and Jackson himself told him, Overton related, "Robards became violently angry and abusive, and threatened to whip Jackson." Jackson responded by challenging him to a duel. Robards then retorted that "he did not care for him nor his wife—abusing them both." Soon Jackson found other quarters. Several months later, Robards departed for Kentucky.[11] There remained now no impediment for Jackson and Rachel to get together.

Much has been written about the circumstances of the divorce of Rachel and Lewis Robards and the subsequent marriage of Rachel and Andrew Jackson.[12] According to Overton, writing years later, Jackson believed that Robards had received an official divorce from Rachel and he was free to pursue her. Subsequently "in the Summer of 1791," they were married in Natchez, then under Spanish authority. Two years later they discovered the divorce had not gone through until September 1793.

Technically Rachel was guilty of bigamy. This fact haunted the couple and provided fodder for Jackson's political enemies for the rest of her days. Upon learning of the unexpected complication, the couple remarried on January 18, 1794.[13] Woe to anyone, however, who dared bring this subject up to the testy, proud Jackson. He was always quick to defend her honor, and where Rachel was concerned, even a hint of an insult produced a reaction. Jackson was proud he had married into one of the oldest and most respected families of early Tennessee, and Rachel now had the protection and love of an up-and-coming lawyer and future military hero. Although Jackson's enemies never let the matter rest, at that time it did not hurt his standing in the community.

As Jackson's social and personal life developed, so too did his professional standing. The young lawyer was making a name for himself even as he acquired land from the cash-strapped clients in payment. Because Jackson had arrived as the public prosecutor, he was immediately hired by merchants and others who were owed debts. These were the influential citizens, and he quickly befriended them and wasted no time in prosecuting the debtors. Within his first month in Nashville, "he had issued . . . seventy writs to delinquent debtors."[14] He represented clients not only in Nashville but also in the surrounding counties. During his first seven years, he spent perhaps half his time in travel, making the two-hundred-mile journey between Nashville and Jonesboro more than twenty times. He was often gone for weeks at a time— many times alone—and thus had to become adept at avoiding Indians. Records reveal that between 1780 and 1794, within seven miles of Nashville, one man, woman, or child was killed by hostiles every ten days. Thirty-three were killed in 1787, the year before Jackson arrived.[15]

Jackson's "first campaign and Indian fight" came after he had been in Nashville about six months. This encounter began his reputation as a great Indian fighter. A party of hostiles had attacked Colonel James Robertson's station, and Jackson with about twenty other men set out after them. Believing they could catch their quarry quicker on foot, they abandoned their horses and set off at "a regular jog-trot." After unknowingly spending the night but a few hundred yards from the Indians, the militia surprised the Indians at dawn. The fleeing Indians left "sixteen guns, nineteen shot-pouches, and all their baggage . . . blankets, moccasins, leggings, skins, and other articles."[16] Although Jackson was only a private, his actions were described as "bold, dashing, fearless, and *mad upon his enemies*" by Sampson Williams, another participant. Both men became "fast friends" and had "a great ambition for encounters with the savages."[17] Because of his bravery in battle, the Indians soon gave Jackson the title "Sharp Knife." Little did they know how appropriate this name would become.

Jackson, along with many other prominent Tennesseans, recognized that they would not prosper economically unless one of two things happened. The Indians had to be somehow pacified so that trade could develop without fear of attack, or they had to be driven out of the area.[18] The other hindrance to development was the presence of Spaniards along the Mississippi. Not only were they supplying the Indians with weapons, but they controlled New Orleans. In the days when river traffic was the only viable means of transportation, access to the port of New Orleans was critical. Through this port would flow all commerce to both foreign and East Coast markets.

In 1789, George Washington became president of the newly formed United States. North Carolina ratified the Constitution and ceded its territories west of the Smoky Mountains to the federal government. Designated the Southwest Territory, it contained the area of modern Tennessee. William Blount, a North Carolinian delegate to the Constitutional Convention, was named governor of the territory. Because of his reputation as an outstanding attorney and Indian fighter, Jackson quickly gained favor with him. In February 1791, Blount named Jackson attorney general for the Mero District, which included Davidson County, where Nashville is located. His duties included not only prosecuting lawbreakers, but also enforcing the recently enacted treaties with the natives. Eighteen months later, September 10, 1792, Blount appointed him judge advocate, or chief legal officer, for the militia of the Mero District.[19]

Jackson, now twenty-five, had his first official position in the military. Realizing the close connection between the militia and political (and thus economic) success, Jackson threw himself into his work. Parton wrote, "The land records of 1794, 1795, 1796, and 1797, show that it was during those years that Jackson laid the foundation of the large estate which he subsequently acquired."[20] The Native Americans, who utilized this area for hunting notwithstanding, land was plentiful. It was not uncommon for a lawyer to receive "a six forty" or 640 acres, one square mile, as payment for even an uncomplicated case. Initially he and Rachel made their home on the Cumberland River on a small plantation named Poplar Grove. Soon, however, he was able to move to a larger estate called Hunter's Hill. It would not be until 1804 that he finally moved to the 420-acre Hermitage located ten miles or so from Nashville.

By 1795, after defeating the Cherokees in the Nickajack expedition, settlers around Nashville felt relatively safe. Jackson does not appear to have taken part in this action. The expedition was led by General Robertson and guided by an escaped prisoner of the Cherokees, who had been captured as a boy. An argument among the tribe ensued about what to do with the lad—kill him or spare him. According to legend, an old Cherokee woman had predicted, "If you do not kill him, he will soon be grown, and will then get away and guide an army here, and we shall all be killed."[21] Her prophecy was fulfilled in late September 1794. Soon settlers began pouring into the Cumberland valley, and the territory would soon reach the needed population to apply for statehood. Jackson was thus positioned to play a pivotal role in that process and reap the rewards that came with it.

On July 11, 1795, Governor Blount ordered a census. According to the Northwest Ordinance of 1787, a territory could apply for statehood after reaching a population of 60,000. The territorial legislature ordered "if upon taking the enumeration of the people in the said Territory . . . it shall appear there are sixty thousand inhabitants therein, counting the whole of the free persons, including those bound to service for a term of years, and excluding Indians not taxed, and adding three-fifths of all other persons," he would call for a constitutional convention. On November 28, 1795, Blount sent President George Washington the results. There were 77,262 inhabitants. Included were 10,613 "other persons," that is, slaves.[22] Jackson was among the five delegates from Davidson County who met for twenty-seven days in Knoxville and formed the new government. When Jackson returned to Nashville, he was a part of the political and social elite and a particular favorite of Blount.

Events moved quickly, and on June 1, 1796, President Washington signed the enabling act that made Tennessee the sixteenth state. Blount and William Cocke served as the first two senators. The powerful Blount wanted Jackson as the representative from the new state and placed his name on the ballot. As soon as he was nominated, John Overton wrote, "I congratulate you on your interest and popularity in this country. Your election is certain."[23] With little opposition Jackson won and became Tennessee's first and only member of the House of Representatives, assuming his seat in December. How was it that the twenty-nine-year-old Jackson, having been in the region only eleven years, could achieve such political heights? Why was he so popular?

Jackson's views mirrored those of the frontier West. By 1796 political parties, which were not mentioned in the Constitution, were beginning to form around the ideas of two men. Alexander Hamilton and the Federalists wanted a strong federal government that would assume all national debts and create a national bank. Federalists favored a loose construction of the Constitution, allowing the government to assume all powers not specifically prohibited. Hamilton's goal was to tie the interests of the wealthy and powerful to the prosperity of the nation. His view was that America's future lay with big business and trade. Diplomatically, he favored England over the republican France.

Like most westerners, Jackson favored states' rights over those of the federal government. For them the government in Philadelphia (the capital moved to Washington, DC, in 1800) was far away and had not served them well. Most frontiersmen believed they were on their own when it came to dealing with Indians and their own future. Thomas Jefferson espoused the ideals of the Democratic-Republicans, who wanted a strict construction of the Constitution. (Martha Washington and others called them "filthy Democrats.")[24] According to him, the federal government should have only those powers specifically provided in the Constitution. His vision was that the strength of America was agrarian and small, independent farmers were the backbone of the nation. Internationally they supported the French republicans over the British. Jackson, who called the Senate "the 20 aristocratic nabobs," spoke their language. He was brash and outspoken. He had fought the Indians, and he recognized that the "Dons," as he called the Spanish, were blocking westward expansion and free trade on the Mississippi. States would settle their own matters rather than Philadelphian "aristos." He would represent the people's interests and do it with all the enthusiasm with which he tackled everything in his life.[25] World events were in motion to allow for the opening of the Mississippi and the westward expansion of America, and Jackson spoke for those moving into this area.

CHAPTER FOUR

The Dueling Judge

"When he came up I looked him in the eye, and I saw
shoot, and there wasn't shoot in nary other eye in the
crowd; and so I says to myself, says I hoss, it's about
time to sing small, and so I did."

—Russell Bean

THE HONORABLE ANDREW Jackson of Tennessee
arrived in the nation's capital, a refined and sophisticated city of
about sixty-five thousand, around the first of December 1796.
Four days later he attended the first session of the Fourth
Congress. A leading member of Congress, Albert Gallatin,
remembered him as "a tall, lank, uncouth-looking personage,
with long locks of hair hanging over his face, and a queue down
his back tied in an eelskin; his dress singular, his manners and
deportment those of a rough backwoodsman" (a filthy Democrat

indeed!).[1] John Adams had just been elected in the first contested election in American history, and the battle lines between the two fledgling parties were drawn.

Jackson soon confirmed the faith placed in him by his constituents and acquired a reputation as a friend of the militia and representative of his state. When Congress adjourned in March 1797, Jackson was happy to go home. He would soon return, not as a congressman, but as senator.

In 1797, Senator William Blount was found guilty "of a high misdemeanor, entirely inconsistent with his public trust and duty as a Senator" and was expelled from the Senate. He had attempted to aid the British in defeating the Spanish in West Florida.[2] Blount, still a potent political force in his state, supported Jackson. Subsequently the Tennessee legislature elected him as United States senator 20 to 13. (It was not until the Seventeenth Amendment, ratified April 8, 1913, that popular vote decided US senators.) Being elected to this position turned out to be one colossal failure for Jackson. Rachel was also distressed to see him leave her again.

"I must now beg you to try to amuse Mrs. Jackson," he wrote Robert Hays, his brother-in-law, "and prevent her from fretting the situation in which I left her—*Bathed in Tears*, fills me with woe. Indeed Sir, It has given me more pain than any Event of my life."[3] This was not the first letter he wrote expressing his love and how much he missed her. Tenderness and even a poetic nature are not qualities that one associates with Jackson, yet he consistently opened his heart to his beloved Rachel. While away as congressman, he wrote, "My Dearest Heart . . . Tho I am absent my Heart rests with you. With what pleasing hopes I view the future period when I shall be restored to your arms there to spend My days in Domestic Sweetness with you the Dear Companion of my life, never to be separated from you again during this transitory and fluctuating life." He longed to return and spend his time with her. This long love letter concluded, "May the great 'I am' [God] bless and protect you until that happy and wished for moment arrives when I am restored to your sweet embrace which is the Nightly prayer of your affectionate husband."[4] Although he loved Rachel, duty was paramount in his life.

Happiness to Rachel was having Andrew at home. With family and friends gathered, a barrel of whiskey tapped, the best fiddler in the area summoned, a lively tune played, the table loaded with food, and a clay pipe filled with tobacco, Rachel was at home. Too soon, however, Jackson would be off again. Perhaps to fill the void of his absence, Rachel found comfort in her faith and the running of their plantation at Hunter's Hill. "Aunt Rachel," as she was known to not only her own nieces and nephews but all the children of the area, visited the sick, comforted the grieving, and welcomed newcomers. She oversaw the prosperous plantation, which then had at least fifteen slaves, and cared for the day-to-day operations. In addition to a distillery, the plantation had a cotton gin and primarily grew cotton, wheat, and corn. Livestock, including Jackson's favorite—racehorses—was also bred. Indeed Rachel was busy. The one ache in her heart was the lack of a child of her own. She and Andrew would have no children.[5]

Jackson's tenure in the Senate was brief and uneventful. The session began November 13, 1797; he presented his credentials and took the oath of office (administered by Vice President Jefferson) on the twenty-second and then we hear nothing more about him. His record in the Senate is a virtual empty page. In April 1798, he left for home and resigned from his position. According to Parton, "partly because he was worn out by the tedium of that honorable idleness . . . he felt himself out of place in so slow and 'dignified' a body . . . he was disgusted with the administration [John Adams] and its projects . . . because he understood . . . General Daniel Smith would be appointed to the vacant seat; but chiefly for reasons personal and pecuniary."[6] He missed Rachel, and his finances were not in good shape. He may also have believed he would obtain another, in his mind, more suitable and ultimately more favorable position—a judgeship.

In December 1798, at the age of thirty-one, Jackson was elected to the Tennessee Supreme Court, a position he held six years, and one that earned him $600 per year, only $150 less than the governor. As a judge, he traveled throughout the state building a reputation for maintaining the dignity and authority of the bench, and "his decisions were short, untechnical, unlearned, sometimes ungrammatical, and generally right."[7] He tended to make judgments with common sense and a strong sense of right and wrong. He was straightforward and said what he thought without using a lot of legal language. In short, he was a firm, no-nonsense judge, who quickly decided backlogged cases—just what the citizens wanted.

One of the most famous tales about Jackson emerged during his tenure as judge. While Jackson was judging in a small rural town, Russell Bean (Parton labeled him the first white man born in the territory), a "great hulking fellow" who was "armed with both pistol and Bowie knife," walked past the courthouse and cursed Jackson, the jury, and everyone else in the place. He had previously been indicted, convicted, branded on the hand, and sentenced for cutting the ears off a baby born to his wife but not of his making. He soon escaped and had a warrant out for his arrest. Jackson ordered the sheriff to arrest and confine the man. The lawman soon meekly returned, explaining he was unable to take Bean. "Summon a posse then," thundered Jackson. Again the sheriff returned and said no one dared approach him because he threatened "to shoot the first skunk that come within ten feet of him." With that news the judge "waxed wroth" and commanded the sheriff to bring in the rascal. He did, and Jackson recessed the court for ten minutes. Armed with two pistols, Jackson confronted Bean, who was in the midst of a crowd of people. "Surrender you infernal villain, this very instant, or I'll blow you through," spoke Jackson calmly. After staring at the judge for a minute, Bean handed over his weapons and gave up. Later, when asked why he had so meekly surrendered to one man after backing down an entire posse, Bean explained, "When he came up I looked him in the eye, and I saw shoot, and there wasn't shoot in nary other eye in the crowd; and so I says to myself, says I hoss, it's about time to sing small, and so I did."[8] Slowly but surely Jackson was becoming a political force in his state. No one messed with a man with "shoot in his eyes" unless he was prepared to follow through. John Sevier was such a man.

One of the most respected and powerful men in Tennessee was the first governor of the state, John Sevier. The hero of the

Battle of King's Mountain during the American Revolution had served three two-year terms as governor and was constitutionally prohibited from seeking a fourth. In a state where hostile Indians were a constant threat, the position of major general of the militia was a powerful one indeed. Sevier wanted that job, but so did the wily Jackson. Traveling all over the state in his position as judge, Jackson wooed the support of the younger militia officers. So cunning was he that upon his nomination for the position, he protested in a letter to Sevier that his candidacy was "unsolicited," and when he protested, he was told that when a man was called upon to serve, "his services belonged to the republick, and he ought to obey the Publick will."[9] He was simply acceding to the demands of "the republick." When the election was held, both men received seventeen votes. Governor Archibald Roane, a Jackson supporter, cast the deciding vote. Despite Sevier's reputation and thirty years of military experience, the thirty-five-year-old Jackson became Major General Jackson of the Tennessee militia, a position he maintained for twelve years until 1814 when he became Major General Jackson in the United States Army.

Furious at being defeated by someone he had at one time labeled a "poor pitifull petty fogging Lawyer," Sevier and his legislative friends passed a bill dividing the state into two military commands. Jackson was given authority only over the western district. While campaigning for Roane's reelection, Jackson wrote an article for the *Knoxville Gazette* implicating Sevier in land fraud. Sevier answered these charges in another article, claiming they were politically motivated. Thus the stage was set for a confrontation between two of the most powerful men in the state. It happened in Knoxville on October 1, 1803.

After adjourning court, Jackson walked out to the sound of Sevier's voice. He was campaigning for governor. A crowd had gathered as he extolled the services he had performed for Tennessee. When he saw Jackson, he made some comment, to which Jackson replied that he, too, had provided services to the state. A visibly angry Sevier replied, "Services? I know of no great services you have rendered the country, except taking a trip to Natchez with another man's wife." Enraged, Jackson replied, "Great God! Do you mention her sacred name?" Shots were fired, Jackson swung his cane like a club, and Sevier waved the cutlass he carried. No one was seriously hurt, but the expression "Great God" came in style for the young men of Knoxville.[10]

As soon as he was able, Jackson fired off a quick letter challenging Sevier. "The ungentlemany Expressions and gasgonading conduct, of yours relative to me yesterday was in true character of yourself," he wrote. "[I] call upon you for satisfaction . . . for this purpose I request an interview."[11] An "interview" was code for a duel. Sevier replied he was ready for an interview anywhere outside the state. Jackson replied, "In the Town of Knoxville did you take the name of a lady in your poluted lips, in the Town of Knoxville did you challenge me to draw, when you were armed with a cutlass and I with a cain, and in the Neighborhood of Knoxville you will atone for it or I will publish you as a coward and paltroon."[12] There followed a series of such letters with name-calling and character assassination. On October 10, Jackson published a letter "To the Publick."

Carrying out his threat, he labeled Sevier as "a base coward and paltroon." Thus the head judge and major general of the western district militia challenged the former governor and commander of the eastern district to a duel.[13]

Finally a meeting place was agreed upon. The showdown was to take place beyond the state border in Indian Territory near South West Point. Jackson arrived first. Not finding his antagonist, he started to return to Knoxville, but then Sevier and his party appeared. Shouting curses and making a faux cavalry charge, Jackson used his cane as a lance in what would appear to be a laughable scene. No shots were fired. No one was hurt. Together they rode "amicably" back to Knoxville, and the enmity between the two was over.[14] The next duel in which Jackson was involved would have lifelong consequences, however.

As noted earlier, one of Jackson's loves was horse racing. In his stable Truxton was one of the fastest in the area and the object of many a challenge. (Reportedly he earned Jackson more than $20,000 in the next few years, and his stud fee was $30 in ginned cotton.)[15] Another breeder of horses, Joseph Erwin, challenged him to a race. Because his horse, Ploughboy, could not make the race, Erwin was forced to forfeit the $800 "failure to appear" bond. Initially Jackson disputed the type of promissory notes with which Ervin wanted to pay him. Although they eventually worked out a settlement, it was not the end of the affair. Thomas Swann, new to the area and desiring to make a name for himself, told Erwin and his son-in-law, Charles Dickinson, that Jackson questioned their honor and character. Basically Jackson told Swann to mind his own business. For some unclear reason,

Jackson believed that Dickinson was behind the entire affair and that he had made a disparaging remark about Rachel. For the next six months correspondence between the two, made worse by public announcements in the newspaper, heated until finally a duel was arranged.[16]

On May 29, 1806, Jackson, John Overton, and three others departed Nashville for Kentucky, where dueling was more freely accepted. The duel was to take place the following day. "It is agreed the distance shall be 24 feet," Overton had stipulated, "the parties to stand facing each other with their pistols down purpedicularly." After they were ready, the single word *fire!* would be given. If either man shot prematurely, the seconds promised "to shoot him down instantly."[17]

Jackson was aware that Dickinson was a good shot. Reportedly he could quickly place four shots in a dollar-sized coin at twenty-four feet. Jackson believed he would get hit, but expected his strong will to allow him to finish the business. On the way to the duel the confident Dickinson showed off his skill by practicing on trees with Jackson's figure outlined and even severed a string near a tavern. He instructed the owner to show that to Jackson if he came that way. At the appointed time they met on the Red River. Dickinson had his pick of Jackson's pistols. The barrels were nine inches long, and the one-ounce balls were .70 caliber.

After pacing the twenty-four feet, they turned and faced each other. "Gentlemen, are you ready?" asked Overton. "Ready," quickly replied Dickinson. "Yes, sir," replied Jackson. "Fere!" yelled Overton in his accented speech. Dickinson quickly got off a shot, and a puff of dust was observed near Jackson's heart. He clutched his breast with his left arm, and after just a moment's hesitation, he raised his pistol. With fear in his voice, Dickinson cried, "My God! Have I missed him?" He stumbled back away from the line. "Stand on the mark," instructed Overton, raising his pistol. Dickinson stood tall, and Jackson fired. The only sound was a "click" as the hammer stuck. That might have ended it, but Jackson was not satisfied. Again, he raised the pistol and fired. This time Dickinson went down, shot in the gut. The bullet entered below the ribs and passed through the body. It took nearly twelve hours for him to painfully bleed to death.[18]

As Jackson was getting on his horse, Overton noted his boot was full of blood. Jackson admitted he had been "pinked" but did not want to let Dickinson's men know. With a touch of bravado Jackson continued, "Sir, I should have killed him if he had shot me in the brain."[19] Later a surgeon reported he had been struck in the chest. Two shattered ribs had deflected the bullet from the heart. Dickinson had hit him just where he aimed, and had Jackson's jacket not been so loose fitting, the bullet would have entered his heart. He carried that bullet, which caused him much pain and suffering, as a reminder of his rash temper until the day he died nearly forty years later.[20]

CHAPTER FIVE

Hostility with the Creeks

"Fear is better than love with an Indian."

—Major General Andrew Jackson

IN OCTOBER 1800, a powerful Napoleon in a secret treaty influenced Spain to return the city of New Orleans to French control. France had lost all its North American possessions in the French and Indian War (1754–63), and Spain, or as Jackson called them, "the Dons" controlled all access to the Gulf. Napoleon desired to reestablish the French presence in America, and the port city was key to his plan. A successful revolt in the island nation of Haiti, coupled with a war in Europe, however, changed his mind. President Jefferson recognized the need for access to the river and further westward expansion for the nation to grow and prosper. Therefore, he sent Robert Livingston, later joined by James Monroe, to Paris to discuss

43

the possible purchase of New Orleans. Napoleon, needing ready cash, offered all of Louisiana for sale. On April 30, 1803, the Louisiana Purchase was formalized. The United States nearly doubled in size by obtaining about 800,000 square miles from the Mississippi to the Rocky Mountains, for the sum of about $15 million. Jefferson's vision of having independent farmers as the backbone of the nation now seemed feasible, and America had its access to the Gulf of Mexico.

The problem with the agreement was that France had never actually taken possession of Louisiana from Spain. In an earlier treaty, France agreed not to cede the area to a third nation, but to return it to Spain. How would the Spanish react? Would they peacefully concede New Orleans to the Americans? A concerned Jefferson ordered the militia in western Tennessee to be prepared to act. Jackson was ready and immediately ordered the militia to prepare to confront any threat to the nation—either from foreign aggression or from an internal foe. To Jackson's disappointment, Spain peacefully left. General James Wilkinson with a regular army detachment took over the city, and William C. C. Claiborne was appointed governor, a position Jackson dearly wanted.

Because many disapproved of the manner in which Jackson killed Dickinson in the duel, he did not regain his social promi-nence for several years. Rachel was a great asset in restoring his reputation. Both liked to socialize, and their two-story, three-room blockhouse was always full of visitors. Known as being wonder-ful hosts, the Jacksons warmly welcomed not only Rachel's large extended family but also visitors of every class without distinc-tion. Especially welcomed were travelers who kept the general informed of events outside Tennessee. One of their most distinguished guests was the former vice president, Aaron Burr.

Burr was popular along the frontier because he worked to get Tennessee admitted as a state and because he killed Federalist Alexander Hamilton in a duel. Thus it was with great fanfare that he arrived in Nashville in 1805. Both he and Jackson shared a common vision—the expulsion of the Spanish from both Florida and the Southwest. In 1806, Jefferson offered Spain $2 million for Florida. Spain refused, and in a letter to Brigadier James Winchester, Jackson excitedly wrote, "The certain consequence [of the failed negotiations] is war." With $2 million he boasted he could take not only Florida but the entire Spanish Southwest. He believed with two thousand volunteers "commanded by firm officers and men of enterprise—I think could look into Santa Fe and Mexico—give freedom and commerce to those provinces and establish peace, and a permanent barier against the inroads and attacks of forreign powers on our interior." Of course Jackson saw himself as one of those "men of enterprise." "Should there be a war this will be a handsome theater for our enterprising young men," he prophesied, "and a certain source of acquiring fame."[1] On the same day he ordered the militia to be "in complete order & at a moments warning be ready to march."[2] Burr concurred, and his presence in the area fit in well with Jackson's plan. He even agreed to supply Burr with five boats capable of carrying men and equipment downriver. Burr, however, was not seeking the country's best interests but his own. Although his exact motives remain unclear, he became involved in shady dealings, possibly even preparing to invade New Orleans with his own army and proclaim himself ruler. Soon, Jackson became suspicious of Burr's motives and sought to distance himself from the man and his actions.

Seeking to preserve his reputation and exonerate himself from any of Burr's activities, Jackson created a paper trail. He wrote several letters concerning Burr's possible duplicity. "I fear there's something rotten in the State of Denmark," he wrote Governor Claiborne in New Orleans. He warned him to keep an eye on "our General" (Wilkinson) and warned of an attack either from Spain or even from "your own Country." He concluded, "I love my Country and Government, I hate the Dons—I would delight to see Mexico reduced, but I will die in the last ditch before I would yield a part to the Dons, or see the Union disunited."[3] He also wrote President Thomas Jefferson, assuring him that Jackson and his troops were ready to meet aggression "from any quarter."

Jefferson got wind of Burr's possible treason and ordered his arrest. After escaping to the wilds of Mississippi, Burr was eventually taken, charged with treason, and brought for trial to Richmond, Virginia. Jackson went to Richmond to testify for Burr. He believed the real villain in the situation was Wilkinson, who, after his death, was discovered to be a paid agent for Spain.[4] In 1807, Burr was acquitted of the charges. Nevertheless, suspicion of Jackson's involvement lingered. It was true he encouraged Burr's activities, and he testified for Burr at his trial. He also built boats and provided provisions for Burr's expedition. His judgment may have been suspect, but his motives were pure. He believed he was making plans to rid North America of Spanish presence. His actions made it clear he was prepared not only to fight Spain to extend the borders of the United States, but also to defend the republic from internal threats.

Jackson, as well as many westerners, thought the Indians were an internal threat that must be dealt with. As early as 1809 he discussed the possibility of removal of the Creeks and Cherokees from the Gulf Coast area with the then governor Willie Blount, brother of William Blount. Blount proposed that the United States exchange land with the tribes then living along the Gulf Coast. His proposal was to "give them lands west of the Mississippi in exchange for their land. " These lands were part of the recently acquired Louisiana Purchase. Although most of the Indians were friendly at that time, any foreign nation wanting to gain control of the area might ally itself with the tribes, supply them with weapons, and foment trouble. In order to avoid trouble, Blount wrote, "I wish them led away from us." His desire was to "act justly toward them," as the move would be "promotive of their interests as Nations to settle over the Mississippi."[5] Although Jackson's reply to this letter was lost, it would appear that he agreed wholeheartedly with the proposal. Not only would the area be free from possible Indian warfare, but it would also ensure the Indians could preserve their customs and way of life—which required large hunting areas—without encroachment by white settlers. Since westward expansion seemed inevitable, it seemed a reasonable solution to a problem that had long vexed the area. The Cherokees and the Creeks thought otherwise.

Major General Jackson's blood boiled when, upon returning from a trip to Georgia, he heard that a war party of Creeks

had committed "horrid cruelty and murders . . . on our inno-
cent, wifes and little babes" on May 12, 1812. Always spoiling
for a fight, especially when those under his care and protection
were threatened, Jackson was ready to attack and "lay their town
in ashes." An example must be made, "*they must be punished*,"
he emphasized, "and our frontier protected." In three weeks
he could have his militia ready and willing to inflict this pun-
ishment. "I only *want your orders*," he pleaded with Governor
Blount. "The fire of the militia is up, they burn for revenge,
and now is the time to give the creeks the fatal blow." He was
also sure the British were aiding the Creeks, who were led by
"*Tecumpsies*" and his brother known as the "*Prophet*." If done
immediately, this revenge would "deter the bad men of the
Choctaws and Chekesaws, from aiding the Creeks."[6]

He also solicited the assistance of and at the same time
included a veiled threat to George Colbert, chief of the
Chickasaws. Jackson learned the marauding Creeks, along
with their booty that included "stolen horses, scalps, and a
white woman prisoner," had passed through Chickasaw land
in escape. The Chickasaws had taken the horses. In a letter,
Jackson queried, "You told us you had taken two horses from
them. Brother, could you not also have taken the woman?" He
reminded the chief that he was his "Friend & Brother," a term
he used five times in this brief letter, and that the Creeks were
also their enemy. He also warned them: "If you suffer the Creeks
to pass through your nation our people in pursuit of them may
kill the Chickasaws through mistake." If they again allowed the
Creeks to pass through their land, "Your Father, the President

will have reason to think the chickesaws are about to let go the treaty they have made with him." Sharp Knife concluded the letter by demanding Colbert supply him with intelligence about the identity of these raiders, where they lived, and especially the location of the white woman. If the guilty were not found, "the whole creek nation shall be covered with blood, fire shall consume their Towns and villages; and their lands shall be divided among the whites—Friend & Brother! You tell us you are the friend of the whites, now prove it to me."[7]

For the first time we get a sense of how Jackson communicated directly with the Indians. He held out the carrot and the stick. If the Indians were cooperative, meaning they did what he said, they had nothing to fear from their white "Father." If, however, they failed to support him and follow his instructions, they would suffer the consequences—their towns destroyed, their people killed, and their lands "divided among the whites." Despite his paternal attitude, however, in the end it made little difference what the Indians said or did. The demands constantly changed.

A follow-up letter to the governor further revealed Jackson's attitude toward and actions against the Indians. Stating that he had twenty-five hundred volunteers and would be ready to move against the Creeks in three days, he replied to Blount's fears of trusting his Indian allies. "I heartily concur," he wrote Blount, "to the little confidence that ought to be placed in the aid or friendship of the Indians." According to Jackson, the goal was to "inlist one nation against another." If the nations went to war, it would be easy to see that "those that are not for us must be against us." He would therefore make the chiefs choose which side they were on. Again he emphasized the carrot-and-the-stick policy. In order to preserve themselves, they must choose to be on the side of the whites. "I believe self interest and self preservation the most predominant passion—fear is better than love with an Indian."[8] He was willing and able to bring retribution upon those who dared disturb the peace.

The ruthlessness that often characterized Jackson's military action is apparent in a subsequent letter to Blount. Although failure to receive adequate arms had held up the general's advance, he assured the governor he would move in a few weeks whether he had sufficient supplies or not. By July 25, "I shall penetrate the creek Towns, untill the Captive [the captured white woman], with her Captors are delivered up," he promised, "and think myself Justifiable, in laying waste their villages, burning their houses, killing their warriors and leading into Captivity their wives and Children." According to Jackson, the safety of the entire frontier required "a speedy stroke against the Creeks." The citizens demanded it, and he would be the sword of their vengeance.[9]

Before Jackson could take his "justifiable" revenge, the perpetrators of the massacre were killed by a Creek party and the white woman returned. Physically she was "very feeble," her "limbs and feet" still "wounded" because of the difficulties she endured, and mentally she appeared "impaired by suffering." After a few weeks of being nursed back to health, however, her "mind appeared to be restored."[10] World events would soon provide the war that Jackson craved.

The real threat to the United States came not from France,

Spain, or internal aggression, but from an old and once defeated enemy—England. The British had never really accepted American independence. They had refused to leave forts on the frontier and were arming the Indians in their raids on settlers in both the West and the South. "War Hawks"—members of Congress led by Speaker of the House from Kentucky, Henry Clay—called for open warfare with the British.

The activists were joined by expansionists who viewed Canada as ripe for the picking to join the United States. Spain possessed the Floridas and would surely side with its ally Great Britain. Here was an opportunity to acquire the entire Gulf Coast. Why should that area not also become a part of the United States? On the high seas the British, always in need of sailors for their vast fleet, were boarding and impressing American seamen into the British navy. Any sailor without what an English captain decided was appropriate identification could be taken aboard and forced to sail with the British. Since voyages could last two years or more, the impressed sailor might never make it home. The powerful British navy also harassed American shipping by seizing cargo bound for Napoleon on the Continent.

On June 18, 1812, the Hawks triumphed, and Congress formally declared war on Great Britain. This conflict, an American failure in so many ways, has been called America's second war of independence. It provided the catalyst, however, that catapulted Jackson into national prominence and removed the obstacles to his greatest desire—American expansion.

THE SHAWANESE PROPHET AND TECUMSEH.

Tecumseh and his brother known as "The Prophet."

Tecumseh (1768–1813) Shawnee leader of the Native American coalition fighting against the forces of the United States military.

CHAPTER SIX

Old Hickory

A soldier remarked that he was "tough." Another said that he was as "tough as hickory." They began by calling him just "Hickory," but as the journey continued, someone added the affectionate "Old" to it.

THE WAR OF 1812 began disastrously for the Americans. Having fewer than twelve thousand regular army troops and possessing a nearly nonexistent navy, the country was ill-prepared for a war. Also, the war was unpopular with a large section of the population, especially in the Northeast. None of the eight Federalist senators, who labeled the conflict "Mr. Madison's War," voted for the declaration. All twenty-eight Democratic-Republicans voted to support Madison.[1] Initially the goal was to take Canada, a target of expansionism since the Revolution. In July 1812, a force under General William Hull, an aging veteran of the American

Revolution, crossed the Detroit River into Canada. He was immediately ambushed by a strong allied Indian coalition forged by Tecumseh. Retreating to Detroit, Hull encountered British troops. The combination of forces was too much for the general, who surrendered Detroit to the combined Anglo-Indian forces. With things going badly in the Northwest, fear of a British landing along the Gulf Coast, possibly Pensacola, Mobile, or most threateningly New Orleans, gripped the frontier.

As soon as Jackson heard about the declaration of war, he offered his services to the president via Governor Blount. He immediately began preparations for recruiting and fitting his militia for battle. "The disaster of the north western army should rouse from his apathy every man who has yet slumbered over the public welfare," he wrote in a letter to the Second Division. Invoking the memory of the words of Thomas Paine, he continued, "These are the times which distinguish the real friend of his country from the town-meeting-bawler, and the sunshine patriot . . . may not the state of Tennessee have the honor of sending 5,000 volunteers to the field of battle?"[2] (About three thousand actually enlisted. Tennessee is known as the Volunteer State.) In October, Blount received orders to send fifteen hundred volunteers to assist General Wilkinson in New Orleans.

In November, Blount ordered the volunteers to ready themselves for the journey to New Orleans. Relying on the "patriotism of the Citizens of Tennessee," Blount wrote Jackson, ". . . each man will be expected to furnish himself as fully as it may be in his own power to do so . . . their own arms and equipments . . . including rifles."[3] Jackson ordered his volunteers to rendezvous in Nashville on December 10. He further specified what each should bring: "The Cavalry will provide themselves with Pistols & Sabres; the Infantry with rifles as far as it may be convenient." Furthermore, each will "appear in uniforms dark blue, or brown . . . of homespun or not, at the election of the wearer. Hunting shirts or coats at the option of the different companies with pantaloons and dark colored socks, white pantaloons, vest &c. may be worn upon parade."[4] Since the expedition was to last up to six months, each soldier should bring clothing for cold and warm weather. They immediately needed their cold weather clothes.

December 10, 1812, dawned as one of the coldest days in Nashville history. Deep snow covered the ground. Since there were no facilities for the more than two thousand troops that appeared, they had to make camp. A thousand cords of firewood were used that night to keep the men from freezing to death. The general and his quartermaster, Major William B. Lewis, were out all night making sure no sleepy guard or drunken soldier froze to death. Around six o'clock in the morning, he and Lewis, nearly frozen themselves from being out all night, entered a tavern. A patron, who had spent the night in a warm bed, remarked in the general's hearing that it was a shame that the men were out in the cold while the officers slept in the best rooms available. "You d—d infernal scoundrel," roared Jackson, "sowing disaffection among the troops. Why, the quartermaster and I have been up all night, making the men comfortable. Let me hear no more such talk, or I'm d—d if I don't ram that red hot andiron down your throat."[5] Although he possessed a fiery temper held in check by a hair trigger and was known as a strict disciplinarian, Jackson also exhibited a tender streak with his men. He led by example, shared their hardships, and woe to anyone who dared take advantage of or criticize his men. They loved him for it, and his manner won him the respect of all who fought with him. These traits would soon earn him an endearing nickname.

In a few days the weather broke, and the army made final preparations for the trip down the Cumberland, to the Ohio, and then joining the Mississippi, for the final run to New Orleans. There Jackson was to come under the command of General James Wilkinson—a man he hated from the Burr debacle. Probably expecting a confrontation, Jackson packed his dueling pistols. Serving with Jackson were Colonel John Coffee, who would distinguish himself as an officer and one of Jackson's most trusted friends; the future Missouri senator, Colonel Thomas Hart Benton, who would figure closely in Jackson's next shooting incident; and Colonel William Hall, commander of the First Regiment of Tennessee Volunteer Infantry. Even though forced to wait until January 7, 1813, to begin, the 2,070 volunteers left in high spirits.[6]

After thirty-nine days of travel, occasionally stopping for supplies, being delayed by ice, and even losing a boat, the flotilla arrived at Natchez. There Jackson met Coffee and the cavalry, who had traveled overland. Before disembarking, he wrote a letter to Rachel. He detailed how well the trip had gone thus far and added a prayer: "I have only to add a renewal of my prayers to the Sovereign of the universe for his superintending care and protection of you and little Andrew." He closed,

"Accept for yourself an affectionate adieu—and kiss Andrew for me—your affectionate Husband."[7] Upon his arrival he found two dispatches from Wilkinson ordering Jackson and his men to remain in place because accommodations were not yet ready for them and no enemy had been reported. Although waiting was not Jackson's strong suit, he obeyed. February passed with no orders. Then he received a message from the new secretary of war, John Armstrong. Believing his orders had finally arrived, Jackson anxiously ripped open the letter. He read, "The causes for embodying & marching to New Orleans the Corps under your command having ceased to exist, you will on receipt of this Letter, consider it as dismissed from public service." In addition he should turn over "all articles of public property" to Wilkinson.[8] After reading and rereading the message, Jackson realized that he and his men, roughly eight hundred miles from home, had been dismissed from service. What was he to do? He couldn't just let his men return through hostile Indian territory without supplies. Perhaps some could join Wilkinson, but that would leave Jackson with a divided and diminished force.

It is the mark of a great leader that he can respond to change quickly and decisively. Although Jackson was devastated and angry, and he blamed his fate on politics, he immediately made preparations to keep his men together and begin the orderly march back to Nashville. What would distinguish Jackson as a general was his ability to motivate men by his example. Yes, he got angry and lashed out at those who crossed him, but he did not do this capriciously. With his soldiers he was firm but fair. He had an indomitable will and exercised tremendous self-control.

He pushed himself more than his men, an attribute recognized and appreciated by his followers, who served him bravely, loyally, and willingly. These qualities were never more apparent than on this trek home. He considered himself more than a military leader to his men—he willingly assumed responsibility for their well-being.

When he addressed the men on March 16, 1813, he reminded them how well they had responded to their country's call for duty. He admitted they had received a raw deal, but they would march home together, care for the sick, and act like soldiers. He promised that he would never leave them. First, however, he fired off a strong reply to Armstrong and letters to his congressman and Rachel.

"If it was intended by this order that we should be dismissed eight hundred miles from home, deprived of arms, tents and supplies for the sick," he indignantly wrote the secretary of war, "it appears that these brave men, who certainly deserve better fate and return from their government was to be intended by this order to be sacrificed." If they escaped disease in this "insalubrious climate," they would meet death by famine. Those few who remained would have to pass unarmed through a "savage land, where our women children and defenceless citizens are daily murdered." Jackson refused to accept these orders but would "commence my march to Nashville in a few days at which place I expect the troops to be paid . . . after which I will dismiss them to their homes and families."[9]

In a letter to Felix Grundy, up for reelection as a Tennessee congressman, he explained the injustice of his predicament and advised, "It rests with the representatives of the state to account to this detachment, how it has happened, that we were thus neglected & left to be sacrificed, by the incumbent in the war department." Armstrong "must have been drunk" when he wrote the order. Surely Grundy would be asked by his constituents how the sick and lame should suffer, die of famine, or fall "an easy prey to the scalping knife of the ruthless savage on their return." Jackson vowed to return his men safe or bury them along the way. "As long as I have friends or credit," he vowed, "I shall stick by them." He would furnish them with what they needed out of his own pocket if necessary.[10]

Writing to Rachel, he expressed his frustration with the government and the shabby treatment it afforded his brave patriots. Then he wrote, "It is therefore my duty to act as a father to the sick and to the well and stay with them until I march into Nashville."[11] He closed this poignant letter with a request to "kiss my little andrew for me and tell him his papa is coming home."[12] A subsequent letter to Rachel further demonstrated his leadership role as caretaker for his men. "I led them into the field," he wrote. "I will at all hazard and risque lead them out, I [will] bring on the sick or be with them—it never shall be said if they have been abandoned by the agents of the government that they have been abandoned by the general."[13] He would do just that, and the men loved him for it.

Jackson's concern for the safety of his men was well founded Upon setting out for the roughly five-hundred-mile return (Jackson had said eight hundred), 156 men were on the sick list, 56 of whom could not even raise their heads. They possessed only eleven wagons to carry the invalids; the rest rode on the officers' horses. Jackson had three horses and gave them up to the sick. He walked with the others. "Where am I?" asked a sick man, raising his head. "On your way *home*!" cried Jackson.[14] Untiringly he trudged the nearly eighteen miles a day. He was everywhere, encouraging, cajoling, enforcing discipline, and seeing to the welfare of the sick. A soldier remarked that he was "tough." Another said he was as "tough as hickory." Initially they called him just "Hickory," but as the journey continued, someone added the affectionate "Old" to it. Thus he received his nickname "Old Hickory"—a name he took pleasure in until his death.[15]

On May 22, the troops arrived in Nashville to a warm reception. A local newspaper, the *Nashville Whig*, praised the leadership of Jackson. "Long will their General live in the memory of the volunteers of West Tennessee," it gushed several days after their return, "for his benevolent, humane, and fatherly treatment to his soldiers; if gratitude and love can reward him, General Jackson has them. It affords us pleasure to say, that there is not a man belonging to the detachment but what loves him." The general had earned a nickname, respect, and even the love of his troops. Had the forty-six-year-old Jackson now matured into an elder statesman and military leader? Not quite. He was to be involved in one more shootout, the consequences of which lasted twenty years.

The origins of the conflict between William Carroll, who had recently arrived from Pittsburgh and was the brigade inspector on the expedition, and a young officer, Littleton Johnston, are unclear. It may have been that Inspector Carroll had angered some during the performance of his duties. It may also have been that he was a northerner, a bit of a dandy, and obviously a favorite of Jackson, who tended to openly favor men he considered worthy. At some point during the return march to Nashville, Johnston apparently believed his honor was insulted, and he challenged Carroll to a duel. Carroll refused because Johnston was not a gentleman and therefore not worthy of the honor. Soon Jesse Benton, the hotheaded younger brother of Jackson's trusted aide and friend Thomas Hart Benton—in Washington at the time—took up Johnston's cause and personally issued a challenge. He was a gentleman, and Carroll could not ignore this affront. Upon their arrival in Nashville, each sought someone to act as a second.

Finding no one in Nashville who would fulfill these duties, Carroll went to the Hermitage and asked Jackson to act as his "friend." Initially Jackson wisely declined. "Why Captain Carroll," replied the general, "I am not the man for such an affair. I am too old. The time has been I should have gone out with pleasure; but at my time of life, it would be extremely injudicious. You must get a man nearer your own age."[16] Carroll persisted and knew how to get Old Hickory's blood going. He stated that there was a conspiracy afoot, out to get his commission, because they were jealous of his favor with Jackson. When Jackson heard Carroll say they wanted to "run me [Carroll] out of the country," he exploded. "Well Carroll," assured Jackson, "you may make your mind easy on one point: they sha'n't run you out of the country as long as Andrew Jackson lives in it."[17] Jackson then rode to Nashville to check into the situation.

Jackson tried his best to stop the duel. After speaking with Jesse Benton, he believed the matter settled. Other young officers, probably jealous of Carroll and of course wanting to see a fight, convinced Benton he had indeed been wronged. Although disgusted by the entire affair, Jackson would not abandon his "friend" and reluctantly agreed to serve as second.

On Monday, June 14, 1813, the duel took place. The two men stood back to back separated by about ten paces. At the command of "fire!" they were to turn and shoot. The challenged—Carroll—had chosen this method since he was not as good a shot as Benton, and at this range he felt he had a better chance of hitting him. At the command, both wheeled. Benton shot first and then "stooped or crouched to receive the fire of his antagonist." As he bent over, the action caused "a portion of his frame, that was always prominent, to be more prominent still." Carroll fired. The shot raked the "prominent portion," that is, the buttocks, of Benton. The humiliating wound took weeks to heal and made Benton the butt of jokes. Carroll was wounded in the thumb.[18]

Even before his return to Nashville, Thomas Hart Benton heard exaggerated stories of how his brother had been abused in the duel. Worse yet, his friend Jackson had acted as second to the shooter. Upon his arrival in Tennessee, troublemakers, including his brother Jesse, continued to put Jackson in the worst possible light, and Benton apparently spoke words publicly that reached the ears of the sensitive Jackson. Letters passed between the two. Jackson demanded to know if Benton had "spoken disrespectfully" of him and even "threatened to make a

Publication" against him. Jackson asked, "Have you or have you not threatened to challenge me?"[19]

In a rather long letter from Franklin, Tennessee, dated July 25, 1813, Benton answered and accused Jackson of conducting the duel "in a savage, unequal, unfair, and base manner." Because of these actions, his brother Jesse "was drawn into a duel against his wishes, and fought under circumstances wherein the chances . . . were *twenty to one against him*." Benton concluded, "I have not threatened to challenge you." He might not have sent out a direct challenge, but Old Hickory, recently the hero of the aborted trip to New Orleans, was losing face. Stories of his involvement in the duel spread throughout the taverns. Ever sensitive to his reputation and public opinion, Jackson "swore by the Eternal" that he would horsewhip Thomas Hart Benton "upon sight" in Nashville. It was only a matter of time before the confrontation took place.[20]

On September 3, 1813, an angry and defiant Benton arrived in Nashville. If Jackson wanted a fight, he would not run. Perhaps to avoid a confrontation, Thomas and his brother Jesse registered at the City Hotel, knowing that Jackson always stayed elsewhere in town. On the same day, Jackson, his nephew Stockley Hays, and Colonel John Coffee arrived and registered at the Old Nashville Inn, their customary place.

The next morning, Coffee suggested they stroll over to the post office to pick up their mail. Jackson carried his riding whip and wore a small sword. As they walked across the square, Coffee glanced sideways at the City Hotel. In the doorway was Thomas Benton "looking daggers at them." "Do you see that fellow?"

he quietly asked Jackson. "Oh, yes," he replied, staring straight ahead, "I have my eye on him." After picking up their mail, the two began walking back to their hotel. This time, however, they determined to walk directly in front of where both Bentons now filled the doorway. When Jackson came up to where Thomas stood, he wheeled, raised his whip, and cried, "Now, you d—d rascal, I am going to punish you. Defend yourself."[21]

Benton reacted immediately by reaching for a pistol in his breast pocket. Even quicker, Jackson pulled one from his back pocket and shoved it in Benton's chest. The surprised Thomas began backing up with Jackson following. Jesse had fled but waited at the back of the hotel. He was carrying a gun loaded with two balls and a slug. As Jackson backed Thomas out the rear of the hotel, Jesse fired. The slug shattered Jackson's left shoulder. One ball passed harmlessly into the wall, but the other lodged near the bone in his upper left arm. Blood poured from the wounded general as he fell. Hearing the shots, Coffee rushed to the scene. Believing Thomas had shot his friend, Coffee fired at him but missed. Realizing Coffee was about to club him with his pistol, Thomas backed up, falling down a flight of stairs.

Hearing the shots, Stockley Hays rushed to the scene where Coffee was seeing to Jackson's wounds. He realized that Jesse had shot his uncle. Pulling out a sword cane, he lunged at Jesse. The thin blade shattered when it struck a button on Jesse's vest. Enraged, Hays pulled out his dirk and with his great strength drove Jesse to the ground and gave him several flesh wounds but failed to kill him. As Jesse struggled, he managed to pull out another weapon. According to Thomas, he "clapped a pistol to the body of Mr. Hays to blow him through, but it misfired."[22] Onlookers intervened and prevented any further bloodletting.[23]

Taken to a room at the Nashville Inn, Jackson bled through two mattresses and nearly died before the bleeding could be staunched. Every doctor in Nashville but one, and he a young man, looked at the shattered arm and recommended amputation. "I'll keep my arm," weakly protested Old Hickory, and he did.[24] The ball was not removed, however, until a surgeon took it out in 1832 while Jackson was in the White House. The ball tormented him for the next twenty years; it was a reminder of his foolishness in getting involved with a duel that was really not his affair. Three weeks passed before he could even get out of bed, his left arm in a sling.

Jackson and Thomas Hart Benton did not meet again until 1823 when they met as United States senators in Washington. They reconciled and became political allies. Jesse, however, went to his deathbed hating Jackson. He also never forgave his brother for supporting his old foe.

CHAPTER SEVEN

The Creek War Begins

"War now! War forever! War upon the living! War upon the dead! Dig their very corpses from the graves. Our country must give no rest to a white man's bones!"

—Tecumseh

EVEN BEFORE THE Benton shootout, events in other parts of the country were taking place that would cause Jackson to once again be placed in the forefront of national news. In 1811, a charismatic Shawnee warrior named Tecumseh had arrived among the Creeks, calling for unity of all Indians from Florida to the Great Lakes and making a case for war. One eyewitness to a council meeting was amazed at his oratorical skills. "His vocal powers and command of the countenance and the facial muscles were unequalled."[1] "Accursed be the race that has seized our country and made women of our warriors," preached

Tecumseh. "Oh, Muscogees! . . . Brush from your eyelids the sleep of slavery. Once more strike for vengeance, once more for your country. . . . Let the white race perish." Even Big Warrior, an ally of the whites during the war who was visibly moved by the speech, was observed clenching and loosening the handle of his blade. Tecumseh continued, "Burn their dwellings! Destroy their stock! Slay their wives and children! The Red Man owns the country. War now! War forever! War upon the living! War upon the dead! Dig their very corpses from the graves. Our country must give no rest to a white man's bones!" Tecumseh then invoked the power of heaven: "This is the will of the Great Spirit, revealed to my brother, his familiar, the Prophet of the Lakes. He sends me to you. . . . Two mighty warriors across the seas [Britain and Spain] will send us arms."[2] Unfortunately two years later these words were put into action.

Tecumseh attempted to unite the Muscogee people. Known among whites as Creeks, because they lived near the myriad of small creeks, lakes, and rivers, they were all part of the Muscogee nation. They were roughly divided into two factions. Those of the lower Creeks, located around the Chattahoochee River in western Georgia and eastern Alabama, found advantage in assimilating with the whites and adopting their ways. The upper Creeks, located in central and southern Alabama along the Coosa and Tallapoosa Rivers, attracted the younger warriors who resisted white encroachment on their lands, resented the mixing of the races, and terrorized both settlers and Indians friendly to whites. In July, a mixed race Scots-Indian, Peter McQueen, with three hundred warriors, fought the Mississippi militia at Burnt

Corn Creek. The results of the battle were mixed. Although McQueen lost precious powder and arms he had received from the Spanish in Pensacola, the standoff emboldened and united the hostile Indians. Fear of future attacks gripped the frontier. Because the Indians themselves were divided in their loyalties, Jackson could exploit this internal division and eventually would almost destroy the entire Creek nation.[3]

Less than a week before the Jackson-Benton shootout in Nashville, a violent faction of the Creeks, known as Red Sticks because of the color of their war clubs, suddenly attacked and slaughtered hundreds of settlers at Fort Mims, Alabama (at that time a part of the Mississippi Territory). Samuel Mims was a trader who had fortified his trading post, making an acre-sized fortress surrounded by upright logs. Discipline was lax even though the day before, two slaves swore they had seen painted Indians in the area. Precisely at noon with the drum beat calling everyone to lunch, about one thousand Creeks rose from their hiding places four hundred yards from the gate and attacked the unsuspecting fort. It would be a massacre.[4]

Under the command of William Weatherford, the son of a Scot trader and a mixed race Indian mother, known among the Creeks as Red Eagle, the Indians charged the gate. Initially the militia put up stiff resistance. At one point a volley killed five of their prophets who had sworn that white bullets could not kill Indians but would split and pass around them. Their deaths slowed the attack only momentarily. "Every Indian was provided with a gun, war club, and a bow and arrows pointed with iron spikes," recalled one survivor. "Some were painted half red and half black. Some were adorned with feathers. Their faces were painted so as to show their terrible contortions."[5]

After three hours, a lull occurred in the fighting, and the surviving settlers thought they might live through the ordeal. Red Eagle, however, appeared on a big black horse and urged them back to the battle. Setting fire to the main building housing many women and children, as well as the outbuildings, created an inferno that consumed many. The screams of the dying ignited the blood lust and a slaughter began. "The helpless inmates were butchered in the quickest manner, and blood and brains besmattered the whole earth," wrote an early historian. "The children were seized by the legs, and killed by beating their heads against the stockading." The British in Pensacola offered five dollars for each American scalp, and so even "the women were scalped, and those who were pregnant were opened while they were alive, and the embryo infants let out of the womb."[6] Red Eagle, appalled at what he witnessed, tried to halt the slaughter but was himself threatened and forced to retire. Only about twelve white soldiers escaped to tell the tale. The Indians spared many blacks and took them as their own slaves. News of the massacre horrified Alabama.

Fear drove many into stockades, abandoning their fields and livestock. War parties looted and burned homes and crops, killed or took livestock, and murdered any unlucky settlers. Disease spread among the refugees in crowded stockades, especially in the town of Mobile. Had Red Eagle attacked the nearly defenseless city, which he would have done if he had Spanish support, he probably could have destroyed it. The Spanish, however, had designs on retaking the city. A letter from the governor of Spanish Florida, Maxeo Gonzalez Manxique, written to Red Eagle urged him not "to burn the town [Mobile] since these houses and properties do not belong to the Americans but to the true Spaniards."[7] Clearly the Americans had to deal with the Spanish threat from the south.

Still on his back from his wounds, Jackson recognized he was the only one who could rally the militia and avenge the massacre, a sentiment held by many. "The anxiety felt on the occasion was greatly increased," wrote an early biographer, "that General Jackson would not be able to command. He was the only man, known in the state, who would discharge the arduous duties of the station, and who could carry with him, the complete confidence of his soldiers."[8] By sheer force of will, Old Hickory would overcome his physical weakness and lead his troops into the field. He would not allow physical limitations to dictate his actions. If he missed this chance, he recognized the possibility of future command was limited. After receiving orders from Governor Blount to call up two thousand militia and five hundred cavalry, Jackson sent out a call to the Tennessee Volunteers—the men who served in the aborted southern expedition—impressing upon them the urgency for service and his fitness to command.

Knowing exactly the language that would motivate his men, he issued a stirring appeal. "Your frontier is threatened with invasion by the savage foe!" he warned. "Already do they advance towards your frontier with their scalping knives unleashed, to butcher your wives, your children, and your helpless babes.

Time is not to be lost. We must hasten to the frontier, or we will find it drenched in the blood of our fellow-citizens."[9] He ordered them to rendezvous at Fayetteville (a village near the Alabama border) on October 4, 1813—exactly one month after his shoot-out. Recognizing there might be a question about his fitness, he assured them, "The health of your General is restored—he will command in person."[10] The general realized he possessed the power to inspire through words. Men responded to his leadership because he gave them clear directives in language they could understand. Although a stern disciplinarian, he applied the same harsh measures to himself. As he left to join his troops, he could not mount a horse without assistance, his left arm was in a sling, and at times of stress he nearly passed out from pain—yet he pressed on.

Unable to make the rendezvous on the appointed date due to his condition, the general sent Major John Reid ahead to deliver a message. In yet another stirring call to rally his men Old Hickory wrote, "We are about to furnish these savages a lesson of admonition. . . . [T]he blood of our women and children, recently spilled at Fort Mims, calls for our vengeance; it must not call in vain. Our borders must no longer be disturbed by the war whoops of these savages, or the cries of suffering victims." The general then stated that unlike the Indians, who waged war like "barbarians," American soldiers would "not allow disorderly passions to tarnish the reputation we shall carry along with us." His army would act differently. "We will commence the campaign by an inviolable attention to discipline and subordination," he directed.[11] Three days later

Jackson completed the nearly ninety-mile trip and joined his troops at Fayetteville.

The overall plan to separate and conquer the Creek nation was fairly simple. Jackson's West Tennessee militia were to meet another army from East Tennessee, under General John Cocke, in northern Alabama and proceed to where the Coosa and Tallapoosa Rivers met. There they were to meet two additional armies—a regiment of US Army regulars from Mississippi Territory under the command of Brigadier General Ferdinand L. Claiborne, and a fourth army from Georgia commanded by General John Floyd. These four armies were to destroy the Red Sticks and build a string of forts about a day's march apart, running north and south and east and west, thus separating the Creeks and providing reinforcements for each other. This entire operation was supposed to be completed in less than ninety days, but due to the lack of supplies and constantly rotating militia, the mission required ten months to complete.[12]

Upon receiving a message that his cavalry, under the command of John Coffee, was under direct threat from Red Eagle's warriors, Jackson ordered his men to march. Incredibly they marched more than thirty miles in less than nine hours.[13] Although the message was false, he met Coffee the following day. Together they moved to the southernmost point of the Tennessee River and erected a defensive position named Fort Deposit. It was to be the base for resupply. He desperately needed food, weapons, and reinforcements, and he believed they were forthcoming. Never known for passivity or patience, Jackson, even without supplies, headed into the mountains after the Red Sticks. "I am determined to move forward," he informed his quartermaster, William B. Lewis, "if I have to live upon acorns."[14] His goal was to reach "Ten Islands" where he heard the hostiles were gathering.[15]

Even while still incapacitated by his wounds, the forward-thinking Jackson had communicated with friendly Creeks. He had long ago learned the importance of good intelligence concerning the enemies' numbers and location. Sending emissaries also to the Choctaws and Cherokees, he discovered the strength and disposition of Red Eagle's forces. The general then formulated his strategy to defeat the hostiles at Ten Islands and move south to Mobile, building a road that fulfilled the overall plan of splitting the Creeks. One of his allies, Cherokee Chief Pathkiller, informed him, "I have spies out constantly, and send out two for Twenty four hours Tour."[16] The general praised him for this strategy and assured him, "It is time that *all* our enemies should feel the force of that power, which has indulged them so long, & which they have, so long, treated with insult."[17] He also promised to support the Indians who stood with him against the Red Sticks. "If one hair of your head is hurt," he promised friendly Creek Chief Chennabee, "or of your family or of any who are friendly to the whites, I will sacrifice a hundred lives to pay for it. Be of good heart & tell your men they have nothing to fear."[18] After dealing with the hostile Indian threat and completing the road to Mobile, Jackson could then continue westward to Pensacola and tackle the real problem in his view—expelling Great Britain and its silent ally, Spain—thus opening the entire South and West to American expansion.[19]

Old Hickory continued his trek to the south, burning

villages and foraging for food. Thirteen miles from the village of Tallushatchee he halted. He sent Coffee and about one thousand troops to destroy this village, a task they undertook with efficiency. "The enemy fought with savage fury," reported Coffee, "and met death with all its horrors, without shrinking or complaining: no one asked to be spared but fought as long as they could stand or sit."[20] Because they fought house to house, men, women, and children died in the attack. Future congressman Davy Crockett, who took part in the action, related the gruesome reality that is war. He and others joined the army months before and were ready for a fight. He admitted, "I felt wolfish all over."[21] Although many women surrendered to the whites, one fought back. Sitting in the doorway of a house, she "placed her feet against the bow she had in her hand, she drew with all her might and let fly at us," related Crockett.[22] The arrow killed a man named Moore. Enraged at seeing their friend dead, the men retaliated. "We shot them like dogs," Davy continued, "and set the house on fire and burned it up with forty-six warriors in it." The next day Crockett and others returned to the village, looking for food. They found potatoes in a cellar under the house they had burned the day before. "Hunger compelled us to eat them," confessed Crockett, "though I had rather not for the oil of the Indians we had burned up on the day before had run down on them and they looked like they had been stewed with fat meat."[23] Afterward Jackson reported to Governor Blount, "We have retaliated for the destruction of Fort Mims."[24]

Out of this destruction arose a touching scene. A ten-month-old babe was found still clinging to his dead mother. Hearing of this, Jackson asked several of the Indian women to care for him. "No," they said, "all his relations are dead, kill him too."[25] Undoubtedly remembering his own experiences as a young orphan, Jackson felt "an unusual sympathy for him," as he related to Rachel.[26] He mixed a little brown sugar and water, gave it to the lad, and sent him to Huntsville where he was cared for at Jackson's expense. After the campaign, he sent the child to Rachel at the Hermitage, named him Lyncoya, and raised him as his own. Lyncoya died of consumption, however, on June 1, 1828, at the age of sixteen to the grief of both parents.[27]

The destruction at Tallushatchee was the first real action of the Creek War. Within a month of almost dying from a wound that shattered his shoulder and left arm, still carrying the ball from the Dickinson duel, Old Hickory demonstrated his nickname. By his reputation and rhetoric he raised an army and confronted near starvation. Through his use of spies and informers, he discovered the enemy position, destroyed it, and gained allies from wavering Creek villages. Victory looked assured. Yet the leadership of Major General Jackson was about to be tested in ways he had not imagined. He would be forced to face down his own troops as well as hostile Indians.

CHAPTER EIGHT

Old Hickory Faces Mutiny

"Mutiny and desertion . . . will be put down."

—Jackson upon hearing his men
were preparing to leave

LESS THAN A week after the massacre at Tallushatchee, another opportunity arose for Jackson to engage Red Eagle. The friendly Indian town of Talladega, about thirty miles from the newly built Fort Strother where his army was bivouacked, was under siege. A chief, under the skin of a hog with the head and feet still attached, managed to escape the encirclement and inform Jackson of their desperate situation. The Red Sticks had surrounded the village of about 150 souls and, seeking to make an example of what happened to traitorous Indians, were starving them out. Jackson could not let that happen and still maintain credibility among the wavering friendly villages. Although lacking supplies and still having no sight of promised reinforcements, Jackson decided to attack. Leaving baggage, the wounded, and a small guard force, he left to confront Red Eagle at midnight on November 7.[1]

With 1,200 infantry and 800 cavalry, about double the warrior strength, Jackson wisely split his men into three columns. This became a favored disposition of troops because it allowed for the rapid formation of a square if the men were surprised by attack. The next evening as Jackson was preparing to attack, he received word that his reinforcements were ordered elsewhere. What should Old Hickory do? His depleted force at Fort Strother was subject to annihilation if attacked. If he retreated to protect them, the Red Sticks would starve out and kill the friendly Creeks at Talladega and undercut the confidence of the friendly Creeks. As was his style, Jackson attacked.

At sunrise his infantry deployed in three columns—the militia on the left and regulars on the right. The cavalry formed a curved line on either wing. The advance guard moved forward to engage. They were then to retreat, drawing the counterattacking Indians into the center of an ever-tightening noose. Initially the tactic worked as the Indians rushed, "screaming and yelling hideously," but soon part of the militia, probably misunderstanding an order, retreated and created an opening.[2] Seeing their dilemma, the Red Sticks took advantage of it and fled into the woods. Although chased by Coffee's cavalry, about 700 made it to safety. Nearly 300 Indians were killed and many more wounded while white losses were 15 killed and 85 wounded.[3] After receiving a little food from the meager supply of the grateful villagers, Jackson hastened back to Fort Strother. What he found was not encouraging.

He expected to find requested supplies from Nashville to feed his nearly starving men. Not only were there no new food-stuffs, but those left behind had consumed the few remaining private stores, leaving only a few dozen hard biscuits and a little beef. These were quickly eaten, and the hungry men began to murmur. Suppressing his anger at the lack of support from the Nashville contractors, the general put on a positive face and "repaired to the bullock pen, and of the offal there thrown away, provided for himself and staff, what he was pleased to call, and seemed really to think, a very comfortable repast."[4] The general and his staff subsisted on tripe, with no seasoning or even bread, for several days.

While all suffered from hunger, a ragged, nearly starving soldier approached the general and begged for food. "It has always been a rule with me," responded Jackson, "never to turn away a hungry man when it was in my power to relieve him, and I will most cheerfully divide with you what I have." He then reached into his pocket and pulled out a few acorns. "This is the best and only fare I have." Of course this soldier related the story to his fellows, and it was soon added to the growing collection of Jackson anecdotes.[5] Although Jackson wrote to Governor Blount and General Cocke, complaining about the contractors, he did not receive what he requested.

"I have been compelled to return here for the want of supplies," he complained to a contractor a few days after the battle, "when I could have completed the destruction of the enemy within ten days. . . . For God's sake send me with all dispatch, plentiful supplies of bread and meat." Jackson then criticized White's lack of involvement in the affair: "General White, instead of forming a junction with me, as he assured me he would, has taken the retrograde motion, after having amused himself with consuming provisions for three weeks . . . has left me to rely on my own strength."[6] A few provisions did arrive, but the general never had enough for his men.

Starving, facing an oncoming winter, the field officers presented Jackson with a rational petition to leave for home. Although starving and wracked by dysentery, Old Hickory, unbending and unyielding, rejected the request and scolded the officers. He now faced a new threat—his men bordered on rebellion. One day the regulars formed up to march home. The general placed the militia in front of them and forced them back to their quarters. The next day the reverse happened. The militia made ready to leave, and the regulars stopped them. Recognizing this could not continue and might lead to open mutiny, Jackson met with the officers.

Resorting to his inspirational rhetoric, Jackson first appealed to their sense of duty. "What is the present situation of our camp?" he asked. "A number of our soldiers are wounded and unable to help themselves. Shall it be said we are so lost to humanity, as to leave them in this condition? . . . No, we will take with us, when we go, our wounded and sick." Next he tried to shame them: "But why should you despond? I do not, and yet your wants are not greater than mine." Next, he gave them hope: "Large supplies are at [Fort] Deposit, and already are officers dispatched to hasten them on. Wagons are on the way." Finally, he gambled: "I have no wish to starve you—none to deceive you. Stay contentedly; and if supplies do not arrive in two days, we will all march back together." They had until morning to decide their fate.[7]

One regiment of the volunteers decided to leave. Jackson agreed they should, and when they met the supply wagon, they were to escort it back. The other regiment and the militia would wait the two days. They passed and still no supplies. The men demanded that the general fulfill his words to march. Dejected and afraid his mission would fail if he returned home and his men dispersed, Jackson threw up his hands and cried, "If only two men will remain with me, I will never abandon this post." "You have one general," replied the good-natured Captain Gordon. "Let us look if we can't find another."[8] Soon 109 men volunteered to remain and defend the fort. Satisfied he was not abandoning his position, Jackson and the remainder of his troops marched to meet the hoped-for food.

They proceeded with the clear understanding that after obtaining supplies, they would return and continue the campaign. That was Jackson's prayer. The men prayed they would find nothing and could then go home. Jackson's prayer was answered. After only twelve miles, they met a supply troop leading a herd of 150 cattle. The ravenous men, although disappointed at seeing the food, halted, killed, cooked, and ate. The beef strengthened not only their bodies but also their desire to keep on the homeward march. The order went out to return to Fort Strother. One company formed and went the other way—to

Nashville. Hearing of this disobedience, the general quickly rode ahead of the column and, with General Coffee at his side, confronted them. The two sides stared at each other. Jackson gave the order to shoot the first man who continued on the homeward path. "By the Immaculate God! I'll blow the d—d villains to eternity, if they advance another step!" Parton fancied him to say.[9] Frightened by both his countenance and his threat, the men slowly turned around. Relieved, Jackson returned to the main body of troops, only to find he had a much larger rebellion on his hands. An entire brigade was preparing to desert.

Acting on the instincts developed over the years to respond quickly and decisively in emergency situations, the general took immediate action, resolving to either triumph or perish in the attempt. Standing alone against nearly a brigade of men, he grabbed a musket—with his arm still in a sling, he was forced to lay it across the neck of his horse—and promised to shoot the first man who moved. Soon Jackson was joined by Coffee and Major Reid. Minutes passed. Sullenly the troops stared at the trio confronting them. Jackson's visage was unbending and unyielding. There was "shoot" in his eyes. Slowly they turned and returned to their duty. Later it was discovered that the musket held by Old Hickory in the confrontation was too old to shoot. As in past incidents of this sort, Jackson's reputation as Old Hickory grew. Now he had backed down an entire brigade with one old musket.[10] The crisis, however, had just begun.

After returning to Fort Strother during the first week of December, receiving fresh supplies, and ordering General Cocke and his troops to join him there, Jackson prepared for a new offensive and quick end to the conflict. Again he was confronted by disgruntled men. The volunteer enlistments were to expire December 10, and they wanted to go home. Jackson believed otherwise. He did not count the months they had spent home awaiting orders—they did—and they were determined to leave. "They therefore look to the general, who holds their confidence," wrote Colonel Martin to Old Hickory, "for an honorable discharge on that day." The men received the general "as an affectionate father" but now desired "to attend their own affairs."[11] The response was classic Jackson. After recounting how bravely and well they had fought, he attempted to shame them. "I cannot, must not believe, that the 'Volunteers of Tennessee' a name ever dear to fame, will disgrace themselves, and a country which they have honored, by abandoning her standard, as mutineers and deserters . . . one thing I will not resign," he continued, "my duty. Mutiny and desertion . . . will be put down."[12]

On the evening of December 9, the men made ready to leave. Hearing of this action, Jackson sprang into action. "The commanding General being informed that an actual mutiny exists in the camp, all officers and soldiers are commanded to put it down," he ordered.[13] Furthermore he ordered his artillery to place their two small pieces facing the rebellious troops. It was another standoff. He ordered the men to return to their posts. No one moved. When Jackson ordered the artillerymen to light their fuses, the action got their attention, and the mutineers' resolve began to waver. They had seen the general in this position before. They knew he would not back down, and those artillery pieces were too close not to miss. Soon several officers

stepped forward and assured him they would remain until reinforcements arrived. Jackson agreed. Again his strength of will
had won the day. On December 12, General Cocke arrived with
his reinforcements. The men were determined that Jackson
should keep his word.

Again he gave an impassioned speech. Again he appealed to
their patriotism and attempted to shame them. Only one man,
Captain Williamson, agreed to stay. Finding he had no alternative, Jackson sent the men home. Then he received another blow.
The enlistments of Cocke's men were also at an end, and they
lacked winter clothing. They, too, departed. As a final disappointment, he learned that Coffee's cavalry, allowed to return to
Tennessee to procure fresh mounts and winter apparel, met the
returning infantry and joined them in their march home. "I am
really ashamed to say anything about the men of my Brigade,"
wrote Coffee to Jackson. "They are now lying encamped with
that holy body of Infantry that deserted you and their country in
the hour and moment of danger."[14]

Jackson now had about fourteen hundred men at Fort
Strother. Within four weeks all of their enlistments would
expire, and Jackson would be a general with no army. He
appealed to Governor Blount. The reply from Blount was not
what Jackson wanted to hear. The enlistments indeed were up,
and perhaps the general should return to Tennessee and wait
for a more auspicious time. A weaker, less self-secure general
might have taken the governor's recommendation—but that
was not Old Hickory's way.

In a long letter to Blount, written at 12:30 a.m. on December

29, 1813, Jackson unburdened his soul. "Your country is in danger:—apply its resources to its defence," he lectured, "Can any course be more plain?"[15] Jackson continued for several pages, criticizing Blount's passivity and encouraging him to act and assert his role as governor to order his generals into the field. "Is it good policy to turn loose upon our defenceless frontiers, five thousand exasperated savages to reek their hands once more in the blood of our citizens?" demanded Jackson. "What! retrograde under such circumstances! I will perish first. No, I will do my duty. I will hold the post I have established, until ordered to abandon them by the commanding general, or die in the struggle;—long since have I determined, not to seek the preservation of life, at the sacrifice of reputation."[16] The letter was classic Jackson. There was no mistaking where he stood and what he would do, and he expected others to do the same.

After sending this letter to Blount, the general presented the case to the remaining men. Did they want to return home? Or would they do the correct thing and remain to finish the war? They chose to leave. Upon their leaving, an angry Jackson wished each "a smoke tail in their teeth, with a Peticoat as a coat of mail to hand down to their offspring."[17] The General had just called all those leaving cowards.

Rachel Donelson Robards Jackson (1767–1838) beloved wife of Andrew Jackson.

A young Maj. General Andrew Jackson

An older "Aunt Rachel" as she was known to the children of the area.

CHAPTER NINE

The Battle of Horseshoe Bend

"Many of the enemy's balls were welded between the muskets and bayonets of our soldiers."

—John Eaton describing the battle

THE YEAR 1814 would see a sharp turnaround for the fortunes of Major General Andrew Jackson. The year began with his army in tatters. At one point, on January 14, he would command no more than 130 men at Fort Strother. His personal physical health declined as he not only failed to completely regain the use of his left arm, but also suffered dysentery almost daily. It seemed his ally, Governor Blount, had deserted him. Jackson suffered loss of both manpower and military supplies, and the Red Sticks had not been defeated. Fresh attacks were reported in Georgia. Just as all looked bleak, his fortunes turned.

Deeply affected by Jackson's scathing letter, Blount sent out a call for twenty-five hundred new volunteers and ordered General Cocke to raise another division in East Tennessee. This army, however, would take at least a month to mobilize. On the same day the militia enlistments were up and his forces diminished to their lowest levels, eight hundred new recruits unexpectedly walked into camp. Although the men were raw and untrained, the sight of them renewed Jackson's spirit. The next day, January 15, an impatient and perhaps even impetuous Jackson ordered the men into the field. He knew where the Red Sticks were located and wasted no time in engaging them. On the way two or three hundred friendly Indians, mainly Creeks but some Cherokees, joined him. He was going to confront Red Eagle at his strongest position—Horseshoe Bend (or Tohopeka)—on the Tallapoosa River.

Six days later, after marching seventy miles, he made camp at Emuckfaw Creek, just three miles from the fortified Creek position at Tohopeka. Sending out spies, he learned the Indians were "whooping and dancing [and] seemed to be apprised of our approach."[1] Since they were also removing their women and children, Jackson figured they were preparing for attack. He was right. About dawn, "the alarm guns of our sentinels, succeeded by shrieks and savage yells, announced their presence."[2] When the Indians attacked the militia's left flank, the general was ready for them.

Reinforced by Coffee, the militia routed the charge and continued on to the village at Tohopeka, seeking to destroy it.

Finding this stronghold too well fortified for a direct strike, Coffee returned to Jackson. Suddenly the pickets on the right flank were attacked by an even larger force. Sensing correctly that this attack was a feint, Jackson ordered the left flank to hold steady. Coffee immediately requested permission to counter-attack, an order quickly granted. During the course of Coffee's charge, he was wounded, and Major Alexander Donelson, one of Jackson's aides and Rachel's nephew, was killed by a ball in the head. Jackson later recounted the situation: "The enemy had intended the attack on the right as a feint, and expecting to direct all my attention thither, meant to attack me again, and with their main force, on the left flank, which they had hoped to find weakened and in disorder—they were disappointed."[3]

A prepared militia force met the oncoming main attack. The Indians fought "by quick and irregular firing, from behind logs, trees, shrubbery, and whatever could afford concealment; behind these, prostrating themselves after firing, and, reloading, they would rise and discharge their guns."[4] Jackson ordered a counterattack by Colonel Billy Carroll, who dislodged the attackers and began a pursuit. "They were overtaken and destroyed in considerable numbers: their loss was great, but not certainly known."[5] Although considered a victory for Jackson, the battle might have ended otherwise. Tactically the Creeks might have been successful. Their plan to attack on three sides at once might have succeeded had not the Chealegrans, a tribe in the Creek confederation, decided it was more prudent to return to their villages than attack.[6] With dwindling supplies and many wounded, the general decided to return to Fort Strother.

Along the way, Jackson recognized he was being followed. Upon arriving at Enotachopco Creek that evening, he formed a defensive breastwork. The attack did not materialize, and the next morning the crossing began. Part of the column, along with the wounded, had crossed when a shot rang out from the rear guard. Anticipating this tactic and even hearing the shot "with pleasure" so sure was he of his troops, Jackson ordered the rear guard to turn and face the enemy. His remaining troops were then to fan out on both flanks and encircle the oncoming Creeks. It should have worked beautifully. To his great dismay, Jackson watched the rear guard give way in confusion. "To my astonishment and mortification," wrote Jackson in his report to General Pinckney, "when the word had been give to Colo Carroll to halt and form . . . I beheld . . . the rearguard precipitately give way. The shameful retreat was disastrous in the extreme."[7]

The artillery company, however, commanded by Lieutenant Armstrong, made a fight of it. Joined by Colonel Carroll and with less than a hundred men, they faced an enemy five times greater. As Armstrong was hit and lay dying, he admonished his men, "Some of you must perish; but don't lose the gun."[8] Meanwhile Jackson managed to re-form his confused and fleeing men and counterattacked. Even Coffee, wounded the previous day and carried on a litter, rose to rally his men. Slowly the Indians retreated before the onslaught of the previously inexperienced and green troops, who were now baptized in fire and rallied by the indomitable Old Hickory.

"Of the general himself," wrote an observer, "it is scarcely necessary to remark, that but for him, every thing must have gone to ruin." Described as "the rallying point even for the spirits of the brave" and one on whom "all hopes were rested," Jackson was everywhere. He halted the fleeing and, "rallying the alarmed," seemed to disdain the "midst of showers of ball" that surrounded him. Because of his example, "cowards forgot their panic, and fronted danger, when they heard his voice, and beheld his manner; and the brave would have formed around his body a rampart with their own."[9] The butcher's bill for the encounter was twenty dead and seventy-five wounded. Several soon died from their wounds. Red Stick losses were around two hundred.

The results of these two engagements, although not clearcut victories, were positive on many fronts. Jackson's reputation as a tough and capable general increased. With little success in the War of 1812 from other leaders, the nation was hungry for victorious heroes. Jackson's national reputation and stock increased dramatically as the *National Intelligence*, a newspaper favorable to the Madison administration, and the opposition Federalist *Evening Post* wrote of his accomplishments. His commander, General Pinckney, also wrote highly of him. "I take the liberty," he wrote to the secretary of war, "of drawing your attention to the present and former correspondence of General Jackson. Without the personal firmness, popularity, and exertions of that officer, the Indian war, on the part of Tennessee, would have been abandoned." He also recommended Jackson be promoted from the Tennessee militia to the rank of general in the regular US Army.[10] Jackson's national standing was not the only positive result.

Loss of significant manpower by the Red Sticks brought the Creek War one step closer to completion. Due to their losses, they were forced to stop offensive operations and retreat to their main stronghold at Horseshoe Bend to lick their wounds. Perhaps most important was the psychological effect on the civilian population. The actions seemed to break the spell of negativity once surrounding Jackson and his men. A military victory, however small, can often raise spirits and support for the cause. Confidence in themselves and their commander soared, and volunteers flocked to join the militia. By March, five thousand troops, including the Thirty-Ninth US Infantry under the command of Colonel John Williams, had joined him at Fort Strother.

One person more distraught with events and his absence than pleased over his success was Rachel. "Oh my unfortunate Nephew [Alexander Donelson]," she wrote with palpable grief on February 18. "He is gon how I deplore his Loss his untimely End." Opening her heart to Andrew about how she missed him, Rachel continued, "My Dear pray Let me Conjur you by every Tie of Love of friendship to Let me see you before you go againe. . . . I must see you pray My Darling never make me so unhappy for aney Country. . . . You have served your Country Long Enough you have gained many Larells you have Ernd them." This heart-wrenching letter ends with "health and happy Dayes until we meete. Let it not be Long from your Dearest friend and faithfull wife until Death." It was signed, Rachel Jackson.[11]

During March, Jackson prepared to bring a conclusion to the Creek War. He began by addressing the lack of supplies. Hoping to increase accessibility for food and ordnance, he ordered the improvement of the road from Fort Deposit to Fort Strother. Whipping his recruits into an effective fighting force was also a priority. Thus when Jackson heard that a young recruit named John Woods seemed to resist a lawful order from an officer, grabbed his rifle, and threatened to shoot the first man that touched him, Jackson became incensed. Bursting from his tent, he exploded: "Which is the——rascal? Shoot him! Shoot him! Blow ten balls through the——villains body."[12] Thankfully by the time Jackson arrived at the scene, Woods's friends had disarmed him. He was clapped in irons, placed in confinement, and charged with disobedience to orders, disrespect to a commanding officer, and mutiny.

On March 12, in the open forest, the trial took place. Woods was found guilty of all charges and sentenced to death by firing squad. Despite appeals for clemency, Jackson was unmoved. Two days later in front of the assembled army, a squad of regulars aimed their .70 caliber smoothbore muskets at John Woods and fired. "The execution was productive of the happiest effects," observed Eaton. "Order was produced . . . and a strict obedience afterwards characterized the army."[13] Two hours after the execution, Jackson ordered the army to march.

First, his army would attack the fortified village on the Tallapoosa. Next, they were to enter the very center of Creek land called the Hickory or Holy Ground, found where the Tallapoosa and Coosa unite to form the Alabama River. Jackson ordered Colonel Williams ahead to build a post on the Coosa River where provisions could be stored and accessed. After a rendezvous at what would be called Fort Williams, Jackson and more than two thousand troops set out for Tohopeka on the Tallapoosa. More than one thousand braves and three hundred women and children awaited Jackson. This fortress was constructed on a bend in the Tallapoosa River and was thus surrounded on three sides by water. Access was through a three-hundred-fifty-yard-wide neck, heavily fortified by horizontally placed tree trunks and large timbers, with only one narrow entrance. A double row of firing portholes covered all approaches. Should the defenses be breached, escape was down the river in canoes prepared for such a purpose.[14] On March 27, 1814, Jackson and his forces confronted the bastion. The ensuing Battle of Horseshoe Bend would be one of the most significant battles in the War of 1812.

Immediately recognizing the Creeks had placed themselves in an untenable position—they were penned up like cattle—Jackson sought to prevent any means of escape. He ordered Coffee and friendly Indians to cross the river and guard the bank covered with canoes. Next, he shelled the walls with his two artillery pieces. The three- and six-pound balls had no effect on the thick walls. Thus occupied, the Indians did not notice that Coffee had sent swimmers across to cut loose the canoes and ordered a party under Colonel Morgan to burn the huts along the bank. As smoke filled the air, Jackson used the distraction to charge the breastworks.

The initial attack was led by Colonel Williams and the Thirty-Ninth regulars assisted by Colonel Bunch and his militia. Although taking many casualties from the withering fire, they soon managed to reach the walls. The fight now was for the firing portholes as each side sought to stick their muskets through and fire. "Many of the enemy's balls were welded between the muskets and bayonets of our soldiers," reported Eaton.[15] Amidst the shooting, Major Lemuel P. Montgomery, with the Thirty-Ninth, jumped on the wall and yelled for his men to follow. Scarcely completing these words, he fell to the ground, shot through the head.[16] Montgomery's troops, encouraged by his words and example, poured over the wall and fired into the retreating Creeks. Ensign Sam Houston, the future Texas hero, was one of those who chased the fleeing warriors and received two balls in his right shoulder before the day was done. Some raced to escape by canoe, only to find Coffee and his forces. Others sought to escape the carnage by hiding among cliffs and hills covered by fallen trees. Others fought from huts, from behind fallen logs or any other cover available. It was hopeless.

Numerous warriors had gathered on a bluff behind a makeshift defense. Believing further resistance only meant more bloodshed, Jackson sent an emissary to ask for surrender. The response was a round of balls, wounding one of the soldiers. Quarter was now neither to be given nor to be received. Artillery was turned upon them; torches were thrown into the brush where they might be hiding; the Red Sticks were systematically killed as they ran from one hiding place to another. Only darkness halted the slaughter. Under its cover a few succeeded in escaping. "The enemy were completely routed," recorded Jackson. "It is believed not more than twenty have escaped."[17] One who did escape and lived to tell about the experience was brave Chief Manowa. Although shot many times, he jumped into four feet of water, held on to a root, and breathing through a hollow cane, waited hours for darkness to fall so he might escape.[18]

Only four warriors along with three hundred women and children were taken prisoner. "None of them begged for quarter," reported Pickett, "but everyone sold his life at the dearest rate."[19] A count the next day revealed 557 Indian bodies. Although the slaughter had stopped, the cruelty continued. "So as to make no mistake in the count," reported one old soldier, the detail assigned to this mission "cut off the tip of each dead Indian's nose so soon as the count was made. . . . The Indians take off the scalps. These soldiers took off the nose."[20] Another witness recounted that the "Tennessee soldiers cut long strips of skin from the bodies of the dead Indians and with these made bridle reins."[21] Including the bodies in the water and those later found in the woods, about 900 Red Sticks had perished. Jackson's losses were 47 dead and 159 wounded. Friendly Indians had a casualty rate of 23 killed and 47 wounded.[22]

With the Battle of Horseshoe Bend, Jackson eliminated the threat of major Indian resistance in the Southwest and hastened the end of the War of 1812. The back of Creek resistance was broken. About half of the Red Stick fighting force was dead. The rest scattered to Florida or went into hiding. In addition, the British were deprived of potential allies who might have provided the means to lengthen the war. Although satisfied at the outcome of the battle, and soon to be even more famous on the national scene, Jackson was still not content. Red Eagle was not among those killed or captured.

CHAPTER TEN

The Creek War Ends: The Treaty of Fort Jackson

"General Jackson, I am not afraid of you. I fear no man for I am a Creek warrior."

—Chief Red Eagle upon his surrender

AFTER HIS VICTORY at Horseshoe Bend, Jackson prepared for one more battle to end the war and to capture the person he believed was responsible for the slaughter at Fort Mims—the elusive Red Eagle or William Weatherford. First, he returned to Fort Williams for resupply and rest. His intention was to proceed as soon as possible to the Hickory Ground at the confluence of the Coosa and Tallapoosa Rivers and unite with other militia units sent by General Pinckney. Indian prophets called this area "Holy Ground" because no white had set foot upon it and therefore it would prove impregnable to attack.[1] Old Hickory would soon prove them mistaken. Before leaving on this mission, sensing his men were emotionally as well as physically spent, he animated them with another of his fiery messages.

"You have entitled yourselves to the gratitude of your country and your general," he addressed the assembled troops. "The expedition from which you have just returned, has, by your good conduct, been rendered prosperous . . . it has redeemed the character of your state, and of that description of troops, of which the greater part of you are." The Red Sticks had expected to defeat the Tennesseans. "By their yells, they hoped to frighten us," Old Hickory continued, "and with their wooden fortifications to oppose us. Stupid mortals! Their yells but designated their situation [exposed their location] . . . whilst their walls became a snare for their destruction. . . . The fiends of Tallapoosa will no longer murder our women and children, or destroy the quiet of our borders." The defeated Creeks, however, had not sued for peace, they were still a threat, and therefore, "They must be made to know, that their prophets are imposters, and that our strength is mighty, and will prevail."[2] On April 5 they set out.

By April 18, Jackson joined the militia from Georgia and North Carolina at the area known as Hickory Ground. Cleaning out an abandoned, century-old French fortification known as Fort Toulouse, they erected Fort Jackson (named of course for the general) and raised the colors. He did not need to wait long before the principal chiefs of the surrounding tribes came to him, assuring him of their desire for peace. Jackson informed them that the evidence of this desire was that they would move their villages north of Fort William—"no other proof than this, of their pacific dispositions, would be received."[3] But Jackson had one more demand as proof of their loyalty—bring him Weatherford, bound and under guard.

Hearing of this demand and desiring to avoid further bloodshed or prevent yet more humiliation to the chiefs, Weatherford surprised Jackson. With his rifle double loaded, in case Big Warrior, the leader of the friendly Indians, gave him any problems, and with a deer he had just shot across the back of his horse, the most feared Red Stick, Red Eagle himself, boldly rode into Jackson's camp to surrender.

Riding directly up to Jackson's tent, he was met by Big Warrior. "Ah! Bill Weatherford, have we got you at last?" he asked. "You——traitor!" replied Weatherford, looking at Big Warrior with total disgust, "If you give any insolence, I will blow a ball through your cowardly heart." Hearing the exchange, Jackson and Colonel Hawkins, the Creek agent, burst out of the tent. "How dare you," exclaimed the general with fury, "ride up to my tent after having murdered the women and children at Fort Mims."[4] With deep emotion and pride, Weatherford answered the general:

General Jackson, I am not afraid of you. I fear no man for I am a Creek warrior. I have nothing to request in behalf of myself. You can kill me if you desire. But I come to beg you to send for the women and children of the war party, who are now starving in the woods. Their fields and cribs have been destroyed by your people, who have driven them to the woods without an ear of corn. I hope that you will send out parties, who will conduct them safely here, in order that they may be fed. I exerted myself in vain to prevent the massacre of women and children at Fort Mims. I am now done fighting. The Red Sticks are nearly all killed. If I could fight you any longer, I would most heartily do so. Send for the women and children. They never did you any harm. But kill me, if the white people want it done.[5]

Admiring his courage and character, Jackson invited Weatherford into his tent. Before he could dismount, however, a crowd of soldiers had gathered. Aware that the target of their hunt was sitting before them, several called out, "Kill him! Kill him!" "Silence," roared Old Hickory. As a hush came over the crowd, he added with fury, "Who would kill as brave a man as this, would rob the dead." He was not to be executed. Jackson knew he was more valuable alive because he could prove an example to any other holdouts. Death would only make him a martyr. Weatherford then proudly dismounted and entered the tent, bringing the freshly killed deer.[6]

In his no-nonsense style, Jackson quickly made it known who was boss. "The terms upon which your nation can be saved," he related, "have already been disclosed; in that way and none other can you obtain safety. If you desire to continue the war you are at liberty to depart unmolested, but if you desire peace, you may remain, and you shall be protected."[7] Weatherford reiterated his desire for peace as a way of alleviating the suffering of his people. "There was a time when I had a choice and could have answered you," replied the chief. "I have none now,—even hope has ended. Once I could animate my warriors to battle; but I cannot animate the dead."[8] A few days later the defeated Weatherford set out to find the remnants of his supporters, inform them of the peace, and convince them to acquiesce. Although some renegades did flee to Florida, and with British assistance continued the struggle, the surrender of the feared Red Eagle appeared to end the Creek War.[9] Secretary of War John Armstrong ordered General Pinckney and agent Benjamin Hawkins to arrange the Treaty of Fort Jackson.

General Pinckney arrived on April 20 to assume command of Fort Jackson, commence negotiations with the chiefs, and send the general and his men home. Pinckney was proud of Jackson's victories, and the two traded award banquets. The last party ended at three o'clock on April 21. Two hours later, at daybreak, Jackson and his men were on the move to Fort William. They completed the sixty-mile journey in three days.

Before leaving for Nashville, Jackson praised his troops. "Within a few days," he began, "you have annihilated the power of a nation that, for twenty years, has been the disturber of your peace. Your vengeance has been glutted. . . . The rapidity of your movements, and the brilliancy of your achievements, have corresponded with the valour by which you have been animated." Jackson concluded the address: "The bravery you have displayed in the field . . . will long be cherished by your general and will not be forgotten by the country you have so materially benefited."[10]

The Jackson who could curse with the best, order the

execution of a young soldier, single-handedly back down a regiment, and encourage his men to superhuman efforts also knew how and when to give credit to those same men. They knew he loved and respected them—as long as they obeyed his commands—and would stand up for them. They also recognized the dominance of his will that pushed him to endure hardship for the sake of victory. He subjected himself to the same tough, unyielding discipline he demanded from them. They then marched north. After arriving at Camp Blount, near Fayetteville, Tennessee, he discharged the men and continued to Nashville.

Jackson received a tumultuous reception at Nashville with speeches by dignitaries, a delegation from Cumberland College, and the "huzzas" of the crowds. Finally he was led to Bell Tavern for a banquet where he addressed the multitude. He and his army had suffered "difficulties and privations," and the "success which attended our exertions has indeed been very great." Yet Jackson also recognized the significance of his victories for his country. "We have added a country to ours," he continued, "which, by connecting the settlements of Georgia with those of the Mississippi Territory, and both of them with our own, will become a secure barrier against foreign invasion." He urged the country to quickly populate these regions. He concluded by remembering "the sons of Tennessee who fell contending for their rights." They proved themselves "worthy of the American name—worthy descendents of their sires of the Revolution."[11]

On May 22, Jackson received word from Secretary Armstrong that because of his gallant and brave actions, and the resignation of General Hampton, he was offered promotion to "Brigadier of the line, with the brevet of Major General."[12] Jackson thought he deserved more. Six days later he got his wish. Major General William Henry Harrison, the hero of the Battle of Tippecanoe and future president, had resigned, thus creating a vacancy. Would Jackson accept this position?[13] You bet he would. On June 20, he sent his acceptance letter to Armstrong and prepared to return to Fort Jackson to command the Seventh Military District. He was to replace Pinckney and follow the same instructions given to him as the chief negotiator of the Creek nation treaty.[14]

Certainly fate or luck played a part in his promotion. All told six generals had stood between him and this position. Through death, resignation, and transfer, these obstacles melted away over a period of just a few months. Without doubt Jackson was the most qualified. Although not a brilliant tactician, he was a proven winner. In about eight months, his indomitable will had overcome tremendous obstacles to bring to the fledgling nation the only real bright spot in the otherwise stalemated War of 1812. He was about to bring an even more successful victory to a war-weary nation.

On June 22, Judge Harry Toulmin of the Mississippi Territory wrote Jackson a stunning letter. Three hundred British marines, with a large number of supplies, including cannon, had landed at Apalachicola and were training and inciting the Creeks to attack settlers, steal cattle, and rustle horses. The Spanish governor admitted to the presence of the British, which clearly violated their neutrality treaty with the United States, but declared they were on Indian land and therefore out of his jurisdiction. Could the general come and help?[15]

Jackson immediately sent a letter to Secretary Armstrong asking for direction. "Query—if the Hostile creeks have taken refuge in East Florida," he asked, "fed and armed there by the Spaniards and British; the latter having landed troops within it and fortifying, with a large supply of Munitions of War and provisions, and exciting the Indians to hostilities—Will the government say to me . . . proceed to———[Pensacola] and reduce it. If so I promise the war in the south has a speedy termination and British influence cut off from the Indians in that quarter."[16] Jackson was requesting nothing less than permission to cross into Spanish territory and deal with them, the British, and hostile Indians. All he needed was permission. Armstrong answered immediately. Jackson should proceed with caution and make sure the Spanish were guilty. If indeed the Spanish were facilitating the hostilities, "we must strike on the broad principles of self-preservation." Jackson, however, did not receive the letter for six months—after the Battle of New Orleans and the end of the war. If the letter had reached Jackson, he would immediately have attacked Pensacola.[17]

Not receiving permission to attack Pensacola, Jackson proceeded to settle the treaty. He ordered a general meeting of all Creek chiefs on August 1 at Fort Jackson. Both the friendly and the hostile chiefs arrived and waited to hear their fate. Even the former were aghast at Jackson's final terms.

Basically the treaty called for indemnity "for the expenses of the war and as a retribution for the injuries sustained by its citizens and by the friendly Creek Indians." This of course meant land, how much was to be determined. Furthermore the United

States could establish military posts, and its citizens could travel freely in the area. The Creeks were also to surrender their prophets "and such other instigators of the War as may be designated by the Government of the U. States."[18] These had been the terms laid out by Pinckney four months previous. But now Jackson was in charge.

The westerners, led by Jackson himself, believed the terms too lenient. They wanted retribution and restitution. Jackson feared that if the Creeks did not cede all the land west of the Coosa River and north of the Alabama River, there was the possibility of the Creeks, Spanish, and Seminoles uniting to cause further mischief. It was a point that seemed more pressing with the British landing. Although some westerners understood Jackson's strategic goals, many simply desired more available land.

The real sticking point was the amount of land to be ceded. Jackson's terms were that the Creeks should cede about twenty-two million acres, roughly half of their territory, including lands from allied tribes; it covered about 60 percent of the present state of Alabama and 20 percent of Georgia. The Indians were impassive as they heard these unbelievably large numbers. They then counseled among themselves. The friendly Indians felt betrayed. They had fought with the whites. Why was their land being taken also? The land left to them would not be sufficient to maintain their way of life. Surely Jackson would reconsider. Big Warrior and another friendly chief, Shelocta, pleaded with the general, reminding him of all they had been through together and how they, too, had suffered in the cause. Jackson was immovable.

He then gave them the ultimatum. "This evening must determine whether or not you are disposed to become friendly," he continued. "Your rejecting the treaty will show you to be enemies of the United States,—enemies even to yourselves. . . . Here is the paper: take it and show the president who are his friends." Those not signing would have to flee to Pensacola and the British.[19] These words stung those, like Big Warrior, who had allied themselves with Jackson from the beginning. They were not "enemies" nor had they been seduced by Tecumseh's vision. Yet they had no alternative. Jackson had the power and dictated the terms.

On August 9, 1814, thirty-five chiefs signed the treaty. Only one had been a Red Stick. All other hostile chiefs had fled to Florida. Jackson wrote to Rachel, "A disagreeable business was done . . . and I know your humanity would feel for them."[20] A few days later, Jackson left for Mobile to deal with the British threat.

CHAPTER ELEVEN

Fort Bowyer and Pensacola

"Don't give up the fort!"

—Major William Lawrence as the British attacked
Fort Bowyer

AS THE YEAR 1814 approached an end, the lingering war
appeared to be a disaster for the United States. In late spring,
Napoleon abdicated his throne as emperor of France and was
exiled to the isle of Elba, thus freeing up British troops to fight
in America. The war in the North was stalemated as neither side
could deal a knockout blow along the Great Lakes. In August, the
Royal Navy, under the command of Admiral George Cockburn,
which blockaded much of the Atlantic Coast, raided, burned,
and looted towns along the Chesapeake. Finally a veteran force
under General Robert Ross defeated a pitiful defense by the local

militia at Bladensburg, Maryland, then occupied and burned the American capital.

When the British entered the White House, they found a sumptuous meal prepared. Dolley Madison had expected her husband and had made great preparations. The British enjoyed the meal and then set the White House, the Capitol, and other government buildings on fire (probably in retaliation for the American burning of the Legislative Assembly of York—now Toronto—in April 1813). Only a torrential rain halted utter destruction.

Dolley Madison managed to evade the attackers, saving only the silver and some furnishings. Most important, she urged the removal of the Gilbert Stuart painting of George Washington. "Save that picture," she cried, "save that picture, if possible; if not possible burn it: under no circumstances allow it to fall into the hands of the British."[1] She also grabbed the Declaration of Independence and fled, assisted by Paul Jennings, a longtime Madison slave. Years later Jennings wrote,

> It has often been stated in print that when Mrs. Madison escaped the White House, she cut out from the frame the large portrait of Washington (now in one of the parlors there), and carried it off. This is totally false. She had not time for doing it. It would have required a ladder to get it down. All she carried off was the silver in her reticule, as the British were thought to be a few squares off, and were expected any moment. John Suse . . . and Magraw, the President's gardener, took it down and sent it off in a wagon.[2]

Sensing total victory was near, the Royal Navy, under the command of Vice Admiral Alexander Cochrane, headed toward the Gulf Coast, hoping to join the remainder of the Creeks, runaway slaves, and black troops from the Caribbean and invade the underbelly of the United States. Their immediate goal was the taking of Mobile so that they could push into the Mississippi Valley, control the river, and link up with forces in Canada. Ultimately the goal was to surround and strangle the nation. To accomplish this feat, they would need the cooperation of the ostensibly neutral Spanish in Pensacola. Unfortunately for British plans, the general on the scene—and about to confront them—was Old Hickory. The victorious general and the emboldened British were about to take each other's measure.[3]

On August 22, Jackson arrived in Mobile. Recognizing the vulnerability of Mobile Bay to British landing, he immediately began to strengthen the fortifications on Fort Bowyer, which protected its entrance. At the same time he made preparations to deal with the British presence in Pensacola. For more than a month Jackson had been in correspondence with the Spanish commandant in Pensacola, Mateo Gonzalez Manrique. Initially he questioned him about the landing of British troops and ordered him to surrender hostile Creek chiefs, such as Peter McQueen and Josiah Francis.[4] Manrique answered that the hostile chiefs were not there, and previous treaties allowed the British to deal with the Creeks on the Apalachicola River. He also countered that the United States should do something about the pirates on the isle of Barataria who were raiding Spanish shipping.[5] The general was unimpressed; his concern was the British farther east.

On August 14, the British Major Edward Nicholls, with about one hundred men, had landed at Pensacola and immediately set about recruiting blacks and Indians. He also invited the pirate Jean Lafitte to join him. Lafitte refused, probably fearing Spanish retaliation—or worse—he would have to cease raiding Spanish vessels and give up some of his loot. Although Nicholls's presence violated Spanish neutrality, a fearful Manrique, acting on his own authority, allowed it. The British quickly so alienated their hosts by raising the British flag and filling the town with Indians that several citizens volunteered as spies for Jackson. In a letter to Governor Blount, Jackson quoted one spy that ten thousand reinforcements were expected daily and that twenty-five thousand of "Lord Wellington's troops" were in Bermuda. Blount should therefore call up the militia and get them ready for action.[6] He also wrote Governor Claiborne, warning of the threat to New Orleans and urging him to get his militia prepared for such an attack.[7] Jackson was convinced the British would attack New Orleans by going through Mobile, and Fort Bowyer alone defended it.[8]

On September 12, four British ships, containing a total of seventy-eight guns, commanded by Admiral William Percy, arrived in Mobile Bay to begin a land-and-sea operation against Fort Bowyer. Major Nicholls and his troops, joined by 130 Indians, came ashore to reconnoiter and build a small fortification. Although the American commander Major William Lawrence with only 160 poorly trained men was seriously

outmanned and with only twenty cannon was seriously out-
gunned, he made preparations to meet the enemy.

On September 15, the attack began in earnest as the flagship *Hermes* sailed into the harbor to within a musket shot of
the fort and fired a broadside. With a shout of "Don't give up the
fort!" Lawrence's men returned fire. Nicholls's land troops also
opened fire, but were quickly routed and forced to withdraw.
The smoke was so thick that neither side could clearly make out
the other, but a lucky shot cut the *Hermes*' cable and set it adrift.
Raked by grapeshot from bow to stern, she drifted for twenty
minutes, finally grounding on a sandbar—a sitting duck even for
the fort's inexperienced gun crew. After dark, Percy recognized
his hopeless situation, gave the order to abandon ship, and set it
on fire. At 11:00 p.m., after burning nearly four hours, flames
reached the powder magazine. The resulting explosion, so loud
it startled Jackson thirty miles away in Mobile, turned the ship
into splinters. Recognizing his defeat, Percy disengaged, and the
remaining three ships set sail.[9]

Several days passed before a messenger informed Jackson
of the victory. He had sent reinforcements, but when they heard
the explosion, they thought the British had destroyed the fort, so
they returned to Mobile. The general was thrilled with the victory. He knew the Indians would perceive weakness in the British.
Concerning the Spanish, he gloated. "What would [Manrique]
now think of his new allies as they crept back to Pensacola, the flag
ship missing, the *Sophia* damaged, Nichols without an eye [lost in
the battle because of a flying splinter], and Percy without a ship?"[10]
"The result of this engagement has stamped a character on the war

in this quarter highly favorable to the American army," he wrote Secretary of War Monroe. "It is an event from which may be drawn the most favorable augury."[11] After the burning of Washington, the incompetent Armstrong was relieved and replaced by James Monroe, who also continued as secretary of state.

On October 10, Monroe informed Jackson that, according to his ministers in Ghent, Belgium, a large force of "twelve or fifteen thousand men" had already left Ireland and were headed to New Orleans. Monroe ordered the governors of Tennessee, Kentucky, and Georgia to raise 12,500 militia and place them under Jackson's authority.[12] Jackson, however, believed he had to remove the British threat from Pensacola before he left for New Orleans. On the same day, Jackson wrote Monroe that the British were still in Pensacola and were arming the Indians and threatening the Spanish. The British commander, Nicholls, "paraded his savage force, marched it through town, saluting his Excellency [Manrique] with the war whoop, and threatened to scalp all the inhabitants."[13] Frustrated at not receiving instructions about Pensacola, Jackson acted—as always—by directly confronting the problem. It was the time to strike at the nexus of the enemy threat, and "by the Eternal" he would do it. It was time to repay Nicholls's visit to Mobile.

"I have been making every exertion to destroy the Hotbed of the war, and the asylum of our enemies," Jackson wrote Coffee, ". . . a moment is not to be lost, to make the blow before they receive their reinforcements."[14] Coffee and his cavalry were to go to Pensacola. Due to the scarcity of grass around the city, one brigade would have to fight on foot. Meanwhile, President Madison, having recently sent a minister to Spain, had other ideas. "I hasten to communicate to you, the directions of the President," wrote Monroe, "that you should at present take no measures, which involve the Government in a contest with Spain."[15] Unaware of the letter, Jackson, without specific instructions, decided to act, and his political enemies would later use the action against him.

"As I act without the orders of the government," he confessed in a letter to Monroe on October 26, "I deem it important to state to you my reasons for the measure I am about to adopt." He explained that the safety of "this section of the union depends upon it." The British had basically taken over Pensacola, supported an expedition against Fort Bowyer, and armed the Indians. It was his responsibility to act: "I feel a confidence that I shall stand Justified to my government. . . . Should I not I shall have the consolation of having done the only thing in my own opinion which could give security to the country . . . an ample reward for the loss of my commission."[16]

It is clear by this letter, to which Monroe never responded, that Jackson had thought through the action and made up his mind. He was going through with his plans whatever the consequences. The letter was simply to justify and explain his decision; in military parlance, he was covering his rear end. Yet he had good reasons to be optimistic. Militarily he was ready. Politically he knew he had the support of the southerners and westerners. Because of past letters, he also believed he had the tacit support of the administration.[17] Moreover, firm, decisive action had served him well in the past.

On November 6, 1814, Jackson with four thousand troops

arrived just outside Pensacola with its three forts. Fort Barrancas was the main fort that covered the bay. Fort Saint Michael and Fort Rose dominated the small town. Jackson immediately sent a note to Manrique: "I come not as an enemy of Spain, but I come with a force sufficient to prevent a repetition of those acts so injurious to the U.S." Jackson then got to the point: "I Therefore demand possession of the [fort] Barrancas and other Fortifications with their munitions of war." Manrique had an hour to make his decision, or "let the blood of your subjects be upon your head. I will not hold myself responsible for the actions of my enraged soldiers and Indian warriors."[18] As Major H. D. Piere carried the message under a white flag to the smaller Fort Saint Michael, he was fired upon.

After hearing this news, the general rode out to the scene and discovered that the fort was manned by both Spanish and British forces. Again he sent a message, this time by a captured Spanish soldier. "Wishing to spare unnecessary effusion of blood," he wrote, "I send you this . . . to learn your real motives on this occasion."[19] Later that evening the corporal returned with a verbal notice that Manrique was powerless to act, and the British had fired on the flag. Piere returned to Manrique with the original note. After consultation with his advisors, Manrique sent Jackson a note stating, " I am resolved to repel by force any attempt you make." That was what the general wanted to hear. "Turn out the troops," he responded.[20]

The men were ready an hour before dawn. Jackson feinted on the west side of town, then attacked in force on the east. "When I approached within a mile I was in full view," he wrote

Governor Blount on November 14, "my pride was never more heightened, than viewing the uniform firmness of my Troops, and with what undaunted courage they advanced." Seven British warships were on their left and strong blockhouses and "batteries of cannon in their Front," but still they advanced with "unshaken firmness."[21]

As the Americans entered the town, they were met by a volley of musketry, followed by cannon fire with grapeshot and ball. Captain William Lavall led the charge at the battery and was hit by grape, shattering his thigh. The regular forces quickly silenced the musket fire. The battle was over in a matter of minutes. Governor Manrique ran around waving a white flag until he found an officer and surrendered. He promised to surrender the forts and accede to the demands if Jackson would but spare the town. The process of surrender took the rest of the day, and by nightfall all but Barrancas was under American control. American losses were five killed and ten wounded.

As Jackson prepared for an early morning attack on this heavily built-up fort, the air was split by "a tremendous explosion." By the time the smoke cleared, Nicholls and his Indian allies had joined the warships and were sailing away. Although frustrated by losing the munitions stored in the fort and not confronting Nicholls, Jackson at least "had the Satisfaction to see the whole British force leave the port and their friends at our Mercy."[22] Indeed, the allegiance of both Manrique and the Indians seemed to change swiftly.

The British defeat at Fort Bowyer and the quick desertion of his allies at Pensacola caused Manrique to switch his allegiance. No longer could Britain depend on Spanish assistance. A few weeks later the British offered to assist him in rebuilding Fort Barrancas. Manrique refused the offer, stating that if he needed assistance, he would seek it from his friend Jackson. He also considered himself Jackson's "most obedient faithful and grateful servant, who kisses your hand."[23] In addition, the Indians became more fearful of the name of Jackson. They had witnessed the wrath of Sharp Knife too often and no longer relied on British aid. Whatever the British now planned in this area they were alone.

Jackson's quick and unexpected march into Florida was a complete success. He had broken the back of British, Spanish, and Indian resistance in the Southeast. "Thus Sir," he proudly wrote Monroe, "I have broken up the hotbed of the Indian war and Convinced the Spaniards That we will permit no equivocations in a nation professing neutrality."[24] Since the British had lost both their base of operations and their allies, plans to begin any future operations in the South had been seriously disrupted. It was time for a new strategy. The British fleet had set sail, but where were they going? Two days after entering the city, seeing no point in maintaining a presence in Pensacola, Jackson returned the city to Manrique and departed for Mobile. After a stop there, he was off to New Orleans.[25] News of his victory quickly spread across the nation still reeling from the disaster in the capital.

On November 15, Jackson wrote his beloved Rachel,

requesting her to join him as soon as possible in New Orleans. In this letter he provided a portrait of a very sick man. "Before I set out from here [Pensacola]," he confided, "I was taken verry ill, the Doctor gave me a dose of Jallap & calemel, which salavated me, and there was Eight days on the march that I never broke bread—my health is restored but I am still verry weak." The fate of the South, and perhaps the future of the United States, rested on this man's frail shoulders.

Although the South, the West, and the Democratic Party hailed Jackson as a hero for his actions, the Federalists quickly condemned his invasion of Florida, fearing a Spanish alliance with the British. They were in the minority. The administration tacitly approved but gave Jackson no public support. After assuring himself that Mobile was not the goal of the British fleet, he ordered Coffee and two thousand men to Baton Rouge, left the defense of Mobile in the hands of Brigadier General James Winchester, and on November 22, left for New Orleans and the battle that would propel him into national prominence and ultimately the presidency of the United States.

CHAPTER TWELVE

New Orleans: Preparation for Battle

"Is this your backwoodsman?"
"He is a prince."

—Socialites of New Orleans upon meeting Jackson

"By the Eternal, they shall not sleep on our soil!"

—Jackson upon hearing the British were ashore

IN 1814 NEW Orleans was a polyglot city of twenty thousand inhabitants, located about one hundred miles from where the muddy Mississippi empties into the Gulf of Mexico. Admitted to the Union only two years before, many of its citizens still did not consider themselves Americans. Composed of French Creoles, plantation owners, descendants of old Spanish families, and adventurous Americans from the East—known locally as "Kaintucks" wherever they came from—the city was both culturally and politically divided. Nearly 50 percent of the population consisted of "people of color," and about half of these were slaves. A Bostonian, John Windship, who had lived in the city nearly five years, wrote in 1814 that "the War of the U.S. is very unpopular with us. . . . If the English should attack us; there is no force competent to repel them." The governor was "a mere nullity," having little authority. Apathy ruled. "It is a matter of indifference to what power we fall provided cotton will sell at $20 per hundredweight."[1] Although Jackson and Monroe had warned that New Orleans was the target of an imminent attack, Governor Claiborne and the legislators were at odds and had no plans for the defense of the city. One eyewitness, the district's chief engineer and chronicler of early Louisiana history, put it bluntly. "There was wanting," wrote Major Lacarrière Latour, "that concentration of power so necessary for the success of military operations."[2] The void of "that concentration of power" was about to be filled.

Into this disunited, apathetic, and chaotic situation rode Major General Andrew Jackson, the very antithesis of these sentiments, on December 1, 1814.[3] Accompanied by his adjutant general Robert Butler, his topographical engineer, Major Howell Tatum, and aide John Reid, Jackson met with a committee from the city. Among these were the governor and the head of the committee for defense, the attorney Edward Livingston. Livingston would soon prove indispensable to the effort as Jackson's secretary, translator, and advisor. His wife was a beautiful Creole woman and a power in New Orleans society. At the end of the campaign Livingston told Jackson, "General, you are the man. You must be President of the United States."[4] At present, however, his appearance belied his future destiny.

Jackson was described as a "tall, gaunt man, of very erect carriage, with a countenance full of stern decision and fearless energy, but furrowed with care and anxiety." Furthermore, "his complexion was sallow and unhealthy; his hair was iron grey, and his body thin and emaciated, like that of one who had just recovered from a lingering and painful sickness." Yet underneath the physical exterior, "the fierce glare of his bright and hawk-like grey eye, betrayed a soul and spirit which triumphed over all the infirmities of the body."[5] His uniform was worn and threadbare, and his knee-high boots needed polish. "His lip and eye denoted the man of unyielding temper," wrote another eyewitness, "and his very hair, slightly silvered, stood erect like quill round his wrinkled brow, as if they scorned to bend."[6] Such was the appearance of the man who came to save the citizens of New Orleans. Soon after his arrival, he addressed the crowd who wanted to get a glimpse of their champion.

He had come, he told them, to protect the city and drive the enemy into the sea—or die trying. They were to assist him in this action by putting aside their petty differences and rallying around the general. As Livingston translated his speech into French, the very countenance of the crowd changed. Here was the leader they needed. Here was a voice of hope. Despair and apathy were replaced by optimism and enthusiasm. His strength and confidence were infectious. Jackson then set up his headquarters and unfurled a flag from the third story at 106 Royal Street, one of the few brick houses in the city.

Livingston invited the forty-seven-year-old Jackson to a reception at his home. "What shall we do," asked the proud Mrs. Livingston, "with this wild General from Tennessee?" The local preconceived idea was that the general was "a wild man of the woods—an Indian almost." As Jackson entered the reception, the startled guests remarked that his appearance was "erect, composed, perfectly self-possessed, with martial bearing . . . one whom nature had stamped a gentleman."[7] During the course of the dinner, the former Salisbury bon vivant and charming dancing student bowed to each of the ladies and charmed them with his witty and intelligent conversation. He assured them he had come to save the city and begged them to put their minds at ease. They were safe. "Is this your backwoodsman?" asked the female guests of Mrs. Livingston. "He is a prince."[8] After retiring from the dinner, Jackson immediately set about creating a defense for the Crescent City (so named because of its shape formed by the Mississippi).

Jackson conferred with his engineers and topographical experts and discovered there was only one feasible approach to attack the city surrounded by swamps, bayous, and trees hanging with Spanish moss. The wide Mississippi protected its west side. An attack from the south would have to be made by sailing nearly one hundred miles up the winding river subject to not only fire from Fort Saint Philip and Fort Saint Leon, both possessing impressive firepower, but also the vagaries of the wind. That left the probable route of attack coming from the east. The land attack, which Jackson believed was the most reasonable, was to come via Mobile. There was, however, another water route. Ships from the Gulf could pass into Lake Borgne to the north and east of the city. This lake connected with Lake Pontchartrain by a narrow channel called the Rigolets. Once ships were in that lake, they could sail down to Bayou Saint John which comes within two miles of the city. This approach was guarded by Fort Saint John, which was in near total disrepair. Northeast of the city was a dry ridge, the Plains of Gentilly and Chef Menteur Road connecting the Rigolets with New Orleans. This was the most logical route, but there were literally hundreds of bayous between the two lakes. Although risky, an attack might arise from any one. Old Hickory wrestled with the question: Where would the British attack?

During November, the port city of Negril Bay, Jamaica, was a beehive of activity. "Seventy or eighty sail of vessels" filled the bay.[9] In command of the largest armada in this hemisphere to date was Admiral Sir Alexander Cochrane in his flagship, the eighty-gun *Tonant*. Almost daily, ships docked, carrying experienced troops from both the Napoleonic wars and the American campaign. General Robert Ross, who had torched Washington, was to command the army. A sniper, however, ended his life while he was leading troops to attack Baltimore. Consequently the less experienced General John Keane replaced him. Cochrane and his sailors were anxious to reach New Orleans, which they were confident of quickly defeating, and capture the rich prize of $15 million in merchandise that was in storage. Prize money was part of the navy's pay, and a prize this size was the prayer of every seaman. The phrase "beauty and booty" became the watchword of the campaign—the former because of the reputation of the women in New Orleans and the latter because of the prize money. On November 27–28, the fleet, with fourteen thousand troops, set sail for New Orleans.[10]

On December 9, Monroe received definite intelligence that Cochrane had sailed. The next day he wrote, alerting Jackson. "Mobile is comparatively a trifling object," he reported. Previous attacks on America had failed, and the British mission was "about to terminate in a final blow against New Orleans." Prophetically he added, "It will, I hope, close there its inglorious career, in such a repulse as will reflect new honor on the American arms."[11]

Meanwhile in the Crescent City, Jackson was everywhere. He inspected the forts along the Mississippi and found them secure. He consulted his engineers and ordered trees felled and barriers built along each of the bayous that ran to the Gulf. Plantation owners were ordered to assist by sending teams of slaves. Lookouts were posted. He ordered Fort Saint John strengthened. His decisive plans imparted a spirit of confidence and unity. The city must make every available preparation, meet the enemy wherever they may appear, and either drive them back into the sea or capture them and bring them to New Orleans. There was no other plan.

Jackson also had to contend with pirates—or privateers as they called themselves. Led by Jean Lafitte and assisted by his brothers Pierre and Dominique, they had established a secure location less than sixty miles southwest of the city on Grand

Terre in Barataria Bay. The renegades, whom Jackson had once called "hellish Banditti," made their living preying mainly on Spanish and French shipping in the Gulf.[12] Privateers carry a written letter of marque from an established government and attack only the shipping of those nations with which the country is at war. Pirates have no such scruples. Many of the most prominent citizens traveled to Barataria to purchase tax-free goods from Lafitte. The shrewd and witty Lafitte once said, "All the offenses I have ever committed have been forced upon me by certain vices in the law."[13]

The British attempted to enlist Lafitte and his men in their attack on New Orleans. He was to be made captain in the Royal Navy and his men would receive land if they agreed to cease attacking Spanish shipping and join Cochrane. Hedging his bets, Lafitte requested two weeks to think over the matter. He subsequently forwarded the letter to Governor Claiborne. In exchange for a general amnesty, he would aid the Americans. "Though proscribed by my adoptive country," he wrote Claiborne, "I will never let slip any occasion of serving her."[14]

This message reached Claiborne just as he was planning an attack on Barataria. He held Jean's brother Pierre in prison and, suspicious of his motives, ordered the attack. On September 16, Commodore Daniel Patterson, commander of the naval forces in the district, had attacked and destroyed the fortress, capturing much booty. Lafitte and most of the pirates escaped. Despite this action, Lafitte believed it was more to his benefit to side with the Americans. Many citizens agreed and asked Jackson to reverse his previous opinion of Lafitte, allow him to serve against the

British, and provide amnesty. The Louisiana legislature issued a resolution calling for amnesty for all former privateers who would enlist in the defense of New Orleans. Recognizing the need for any assistance available—and the privateers had about one thousand seasoned men, shot, flints, and powder—Jackson accepted. In the coming days he would be glad he did.[15]

On December 10, 1814, the British fleet set eyes on the American coast and anchored at the entrance to Lake Borgne. Only five American gunboats protected the lake and floated between Cochrane and his plan to ferry his troops the sixty miles across the lake. From there they could move up Bayou Bienvenue and attack the city by land. Or they could pass through the Rigolets to Lake Pontchartrain and do the same. Recognizing the British intent, but stymied by lack of wind, the American commander Lieutenant Thomas Jones, with his 183 men and 23 guns, attempted to stop him. He drew his tiny gunboats up to face the oncoming force of 45 barges, 1,200 men, and 43 guns—ranging from twelve- to twenty-four-pounders—commanded by Captain Lockyer. The British tars had rowed for thirty-six straight hours. Before attacking the Americans, the flotilla stopped, and the men ate lunch, and rested one hour. Fatigued, and with the wind and tide against them, still the British tars roared "a lusty cheer, [and] they moved steadily onward in one extended line."[16] Although Jones put up a fight, he was overwhelmed by the greater force and surrendered. The victorious British next went ashore, captured several American pickets, and established a base at the mouth of Bayou Bienvenue.[17]

With the loss of the gunboats Jackson lost his eyes and ears on the lake. The British now commanded all access to Lake Borgne and consequently could come up any of the myriad of bayous or canals approaching the city. Old Hickory was forced to increase his defensive positions along these waterways. He also lacked sea communication with Mobile. There was one positive result from the capture of both the American sailors and the pickets, however. Whether by design or through ignorance, the captives exaggerated the number of American troops in the city, which may have numbered around four thousand. They informed the British it was more than four times that number.[18]

After hearing the British controlled the lake, the population of New Orleans panicked. Many fled the city while others milled about wringing their hands. British sympathizers and spies were everywhere. On December 16 in an effort to bring order to the city, Jackson declared martial law, and all citizens were subject to military authority. All who entered the city must appear before the adjutant general's office; all who left needed written permission; no boats could leave New Orleans or Bayou Saint John without written authority; anyone out after 9:00 p.m. without permission would be treated as a spy and held.[19] Civilians were to follow the same rules as soldiers. The strict measure was greeted with approval, and once again fears were calmed.

With Lake Borgne cleared of American presence the British made their move. For nearly a week the British ferried eighteen hundred men from their ships to Pea Island, thirty miles into Lake Borgne. On December 23, the leader of these forces, General Keane, landed at the mouth of Bayou Bienvenue without opposition and began moving toward the city nearly eight miles away. Why this particular bayou was unguarded is a mystery. As the swampy ground became more solid, the British came upon a plantation.

Sitting on his front porch, quietly enjoying a cigar, was Major Gabriel Villere, the son of General Jacques Villere, the owner of the plantation. Suddenly he spotted a line of redcoats approaching. Quickly realizing what was happening, he ran to escape out the back door, only to be met by Colonel William Thornton holding a drawn sword. Villere and his brother Celestin were taken prisoner and closely guarded, awaiting General Keane. Determined to warn Jackson, the major jumped through a window and amid a hail of bullets ran and leaped over a picket fence. "Catch or kill him!" he heard Thornton order. Hearing the pursuers coming upon him, Villere sought a place to hide. At a large live oak, he determined to climb and hide in its branches. Suddenly he heard a low whine at his feet. It was his faithful setter. He knew the dog would betray his presence. Understanding the importance of his message, reluctantly and with tears in his eyes, he took a large stick and killed the dog. After hiding the body, he climbed the tree and waited until the troops had passed. He then hurried to alert the city of the coming invasion while Keane made the Villere plantation his headquarters.[20]

On the afternoon of December 23, Jackson was at work in his headquarters on Royal Street when he heard the sound of galloping horses. Major Villere and two associates burst into his office. "Jackson had barely the strength to stand erect without support," described the biographer Alexander Walker. "His body was sustained alone by the spirit within. Ordinary men would have shrunk into feeble imbeciles, or useless invalids under such a pressure." He still suffered from the dysentery contracted in Alabama. "Reduced to a mere skeleton," continued Walker, "unable to digest his food, and unrefreshed by sleep, his life seemed to be preserved by some miraculous agency."[21] "What news do you bring?" asked the general. "Important! Highly important!" replied Mr. De la Croix, who accompanied Villere. "The British have arrived at Villere's plantation, nine miles below the city, and are there encamped." Villere then described what had happened. Jackson drew himself erect and with "an eye of fire" slammed his fist on the table and exclaimed, "By the Eternal, they shall not sleep on our soil!" After providing the messengers with a glass of wine, he addressed his officers, "Gentlemen, the British are below, we must fight them to-night."[22] The sick, emaciated general again willed himself to battle. "I will smash them," he roared, "so help me God!"[23] Thus was the stage set for the most important and defining battle in the history of the new republic.

The British defeat at the Battle of New Orleans, January 8, 1815.

Jackson and his ragtag band of Americans defeats the British under Sir Edward Packenham.

CHAPTER THIRTEEN

The Battle of New Orleans: Beginnings

"Now, damn their eyes, give it to them!"

—Order for the *Carolina* to begin firing

WITH HIS IMMEDIATE, aggressive, and decisive action, Old Hickory would save the city of New Orleans, thereby assuring American possession of the Southwest and demonstrating to the world that this nation was capable of defeating a major European power on its own. "For it cannot be doubted," chronicled Latour, "but that the enemy, had he not been attacked with such impetuosity [by Jackson]," would not have been able to withstand the charge of "disciplined troops, accustomed to the use of the bayonet."[1] When faced with an immediate threat requiring rapid decision making, Jackson was at his best.

Not so the British General Keane. Believing the informers that the Americans had perhaps twenty thousand troops, he decided to await reinforcements. This hesitation cost him the taking of New Orleans. His men set up camp and in the cold, damp swamp built bonfires to keep warm and dry themselves out. Darkness settled in early on that December night, and by seven o'clock, moonlight was the only guide. The British silhouettes stood out against the fires, making easy targets.

Jackson's plan was to attack the enemy camp from both sides simultaneously. He ordered Commodore Patterson to bring the schooner *Carolina* down the Mississippi. The larger *Louisiana* was unable to maneuver for lack of wind but was to follow as soon as possible. When it was directly opposite the enemy camp, the *Carolina* was to fire a broadside, two twelve-pounders and five sixes, into the British position. The land forces would then attack. Jackson reached sight of the enemy just as darkness fell.[2]

General Coffee, along with Colonel Hind's dragoons and Captain Bell's riflemen, took up position on the edge of a cypress swamp on Jackson's extreme left. Their mission was to drive the British right flank toward the river and the awaiting guns of the *Carolina*. The regular forces, along with Major John Plauche's city volunteers and Major Jean Daguin's black troops, all commanded by Jackson himself, moved down the river. The artillery, under Lieutenant Spoots, guarded the road to the city. This entire force numbered about two thousand, while Keane had eighteen hundred—none of whom expected an American attack.[3]

Around seven thirty, the British heard a "sonorous voice . . .

as if rising out of the waters of the Mississippi, Now, damn their eyes, give it to them!" followed by the roar of seven cannon firing round shot and grape into their midst.[4] Although British pickets had seen the schooner, they paid it little heed, believing it to be just another commercial vessel. For ninety minutes shot after shot poured into the British camp at point-blank range. Initially the British fired rockets at the ship, but these inaccurate weapons had no effect. The *Carolina*'s broadside, followed by a red, white, and blue rocket, was the signal for the land troops to attack.[5]

The surprised redcoats did not know what hit them. Cannon shot at them from the river, and then Coffee's troops descended upon their right. Jackson's main force, set perpendicular to the river, came at their left flank. Tired soldiers tried to get dressed and grab their weapons as bugles sounded. Officers shouted commands as guns flashed in the darkness, felling men, horses, and standing equipment. The experienced Colonel Thornton quickly took command of the situation and ordered troops to support both fronts, while he sent some back to Villere's house as reserve.

A thick fog emerged from the river and mixed with the powder smoke to make the situation even more chaotic. Units became separated, and hand-to-hand fighting began, even as the British counterattacked. "Such confusion took place as seldom occurs in war," wrote British soldier John Henry Cooke. "The bayonet of the British and the knife of the American were in active opposition at close quarters during this eventful night." Due to the darkness and closeness of the action, men called out, "Don't shoot! I'm a friend!" only to be captured by the opposite side.

At one point a British subaltern reported about 120 Americans were taken: "The little corps thus captured consisted mainly of members of the legal profession. The barristers, attorneys, and notaries of New Orleans . . . were all made prisoners." Both sides found this most amusing.[6]

At about five in the morning, frustrated by the fog and confusion of the battlefield and fearing to lose men under such conditions, Jackson ordered withdrawal. He encamped two miles closer to the city behind the Rodriguez canal and awaited the Kentucky militia.[7] American losses were 24 killed, 115 wounded, and 74 taken prisoners.[8] The British lost 46 killed and 167 wounded, with 64 captured.[9] Although losses on both sides were roughly equivalent, Jackson gained the advantage by buying time and making the British believe his forces were greater than they were. Both sides awaited reinforcements. Jackson also began to fortify his position behind the canal.

Old Hickory desperately wanted to again attack at daybreak. He learned, however, that Keane had received another thirty-five hundred men. Listening to the advice of locals who knew the area well, Jackson decided his smaller force of mainly inexperienced militia would not do well in the open against such a force. His best option was to build a defensive position and await the British. "Jackson listened to this advice," wrote an insightful eyewitness, Vincent Nolte, "highly as we may praise the merit of his unwearied energy, perseverance, and intrepidity, his self command on such an occasion is worthy of still loftier praise, as it was a quality which he did not always exhibit during the course of his life."[10] December 24 saw both sides eyeing each other. Only the *Carolina*, now joined by the larger *Louisiana*, continued to harass the British bivouac with its cannon. Neither side, of course, knew that on that very day, the American and British delegations in Ghent, Belgium, had signed the treaty ending the war.[11]

Jackson, however, was not idle. He requisitioned every available tool in the city and began to deepen and widen the Rodriguez canal and erect a barricade behind it. This barrier extended from the east bank of the river to a cypress swamp, nearly three-quarters of a mile away. Slaves were also brought in for this backbreaking work. The workers used cypress logs, empty sugar casks, and barrels to create a framework along the canal. They then filled this in with dirt and mud. By the end of the week the barricade reached at least seven feet in height, and the canal was ten feet wide and perhaps three feet deep. Eventually it would be twenty feet wide in places.[12] In this manner the troops spent Christmas Eve.

The next day, Christmas 1814, a sound of great cheering as well as salvos of cannon came from the British lines. Observers discovered that a new general—not the Duke of Wellington as many believed but Sir Edward Pakenham—had arrived with three thousand fresh troops and assumed command from the incompetent Keane. When he heard the news, Jackson was unimpressed. For hours he rode up and down the line encouraging the men to keep working. "Here," he directed the men, "we shall plant our stakes, and not abandon them until we drive these red-coat rascals into the river, or the swamp."[13]

The veteran thirty-seven-year-old Pakenham was not

pleased with Keane's report of the action thus far or the position of the British troops. On his left was the Mississippi, eight hundred to one thousand yards wide; on his right was an impassable swamp; in front was the American line, about three quarters of a mile long; to his rear were boats that could carry only a third of his forces away if needed. They were in a virtual cul-de-sac.[14] After reconnoitering the American line and seeing no visible army, he decided to press the issue and take the enemy by storm, starting with the pesky fire from the ships.

For two days sailors hauled nine field pieces, two howitzers, one mortar, and a furnace for heating balls the sixty miles from the ships on Lake Borgne through mud, bayous, and swamps to the bank of the river. Noting the British activity, the schooner attempted to get out of the range of these guns—to no avail. The wind was against her. Shot heated red hot in the furnace lodged into the *Carolina*, and in minutes the fire reached the powder magazine. Jackson, in his headquarters at the McCarty mansion two hundred yards behind the embankment, heard the tremendous explosion. Thankfully, all but one of the crew escaped. British soldiers raised a great cheer to see the end of what had plagued them for days. Seeing the danger, the *Louisiana* tried to move upriver. Again the problem was the wind. The Baratarian pirates, however, moved into rowboats and pulled her out of range.[15]

Jackson continued to dig the canal deeper and pile the mud higher on his defensive wall. At the suggestion of Jean Lafitte, who soon became one of Jackson's most trusted and capable aides, he lengthened the wall into the cypress swamp. He also began building batteries with wood platforms surrounded by cotton bales.[16] Also at Lafitte's suggestion, two of the batteries were manned by Renato Beluche and Dominique You, two of the best Baratarian gunners. On the west bank of the river, Patterson established a marine battery with guns from the *Louisiana*.

Pakenham also brought up his artillery. Again with herculean effort the British moved seventeen guns, capable of throwing three hundred pounds per broadside, into position seven hundred yards from the American line. On January 1, 1815, he was ready to attack.[17] At ten o'clock, after the fog lifted, the air was filled with the hissing and whirling sound of Congreve rockets. Although they were inaccurate, the sound and sight of these rockets usually sent an enemy army into panic. Not so with the Americans. "Pay no attention to the rockets boys," calmly called out Jackson. "They are mere toys to amuse children."[18] The Chinese had used rockets fired from bamboo tubes as early as 1232. Sir William Congreve improved upon the use of rockets, and they were used in early nineteenth-century European warfare. In America they were used at Bladensburg and the bombardment of Fort McHenry. Francis Scott Key mentioned them—"And the rockets' red glare"—in "The Star-Spangled Banner."[19] For several hours the bombardment by both sides continued rattling the entire delta. Soon, however, the excellent aim of both the Baratarians and Patterson took its toll, knocking out most of the British guns before they retired from the field. Pakenham realized he would need to make a full-on frontal assault to dislodge the Americans behind the barrier along Rodriguez canal.

There was relatively little action between January 1 and

January 8, but neither side was idle. Jackson built two more lines of defense between the one on the Rodriguez canal, which he continued to improve, and the city. Fifteen hundred more Louisiana militia arrived on January 1, and the next day 2,250 troops from Kentucky added to the American forces. Unfortunately less than half had weapons. Upon his arrival in the city, Jackson had ordered arms for his men. They had not yet arrived, however, and he was furious. The contractor had sent the arms from Pittsburgh on a slow flatboat instead of a steamboat and had stopped to trade along the way. In a letter to Monroe, Jackson complained about not receiving weapons. "Depend upon it," he threatened, "this supiness, this negligence, this *criminality*, let me call it . . . must finally lead, if it is not corrected, to the defeat of our armies and to the disgrace of those who superintend them." A search of the city found only four hundred muskets.[20] Jackson also lacked cannonballs. "By the Almighty God," he screamed at Governor Claiborne, "if you do not send me balls and powder instantly, I shall chop off your head and have it rammed into one of those field pieces."[21] The governor could not provide what he did not have. On the British side, Pakenham awaited the arrival of two thousand additional troops under General John Lambert, including the Seventh Fusiliers and the Forty-Third Regiment. These reinforcements would swell his force to eight thousand trained, well-equipped, and veteran troops. As night fell on January 7, the pieces fell into place for a decisive encounter.

CHAPTER FOURTEEN

New Orleans: The Battle of January 8, 1815

"Give it to them boys; let us finish the business today."

—Jackson's orders upon seeing the advancing British

PAKENHAM HAD DECIDED to ferry Colonel William Thornton with fifteen hundred men to the west bank of the Mississippi. Their mission was to overrun General Morgan's five hundred Louisiana militia, then capture Patterson's battery of twenty-four-pounders. Thornton could then turn the guns on Jackson and catch him in crossfire. His problem was that Villere Canal was not navigable. The barges at Bayou Bienvenue could not get to the river. At Admiral Cochrane's suggestion, Pakenham ordered the canal deepened and widened. This took several days of backbreaking work, but was accomplished on the seventh.

Also on that day Commodore Patterson, noticing the increased British activity, went to have a look across the river. Immediately he recognized the danger. After consulting with Morgan, he knew his troops were no match for the heavy artillery and troops he faced. "Should they cross to-night," he immediately wrote to Jackson, "and only the Force at present on this side to oppose them, they must succeed."[1] He begged Jackson to send reinforcements. The courier, R. D. Shepherd, arrived at headquarters at one in the morning.

Jackson lay asleep on a couch, surrounded by his men, who slept on the floor. "Who's there?" barked a startled Jackson as Shepherd entered. After giving his name, Shepherd delivered his message, assuring the general that Patterson and Morgan believed the main attack would be made on the west bank. "Hurry back," ordered Jackson as he arose, "and tell General Morgan that he is mistaken. The main attack will be on this side and I have no men to spare. He must maintain his position at all hazards." After looking at his watch, he addressed his sleeping aides: "Gentlemen, we have slept enough. Arise. The enemy will be upon us in a few minutes."[2] He did, however, send a few hundred poorly armed Kentuckians to assist Morgan.

At the same time Major General Gibbs was preparing his twenty-two hundred men to attack the American center. Due to faulty intelligence, Pakenham believed this to be the weakest part of the line; in reality it was the strongest. Although cold, tired, wet, and hungry, the British formed into lines as they had been trained to do. Undoubtedly many fixed their thoughts on the "beauty and booty" they expected at the end of that day.

Lieutenant Colonel Thomas Mullens, the son of a lord, led the Forty-Fourth Regiment. His was to be the spearhead of the mission. Their duty was to bring fascines (stalks of sugarcane tied together to serve as a sort of bridge over the canal) and ladders to breach the walls. Likewise, Major General Keane prepared his twelve hundred troops to make a feint on the east side of the river, hoping to draw the fire of Jackson's heavy artillery away from Gibbs. A regiment of blacks from the West Indies would enter the woods and distract Coffee's men and the Choctaws who defended that area. About seven hundred yards from the American line, engineers placed a battery of six eighteen-pounders. Major General Lambert waited in the rear center with fourteen hundred reserves.[3] The attack was to commence when Gibbs heard Thornton's troops engage on the west bank of the river.

Learning from scouts that the British were preparing for attack, and hearing noise behind the enemy lines, few of the approximately four thousand American troops on the front line slept that night. Shortly after one o'clock, Old Hickory, accompanied by his aides, surveyed the situation. The Seventh Regiment, led by Colonel George Ross, was on the east side of the river. On their left was a battalion of the city's militia, under the command of Major Jean Plauche. To their left were the free black battalions, commanded by Pierre Lacoste and Jean Daquin. Next was the very heart of the defense, the Tennessee Forty-Fourth Regiment led by General William Carroll. He was supported by General John Adair, who commanded one thousand Kentuckians. Finally Coffee's cavalry finished the line up to the swampy woods. Choctaws scouted in the swamp. Eight batteries of artillery supported this formidable line of infantry. Number one was only seventy feet from the river, and number eight was on the edge of the swamp.[4] Both sides waited in the dense fog for the signal to begin the attack.

Pakenham waited to hear the fire from Thornton's forces that he had crossed the river and engaged Morgan. He would wait in vain. In an ominous warning of what was to come, the swift current took those troops that made it across the river to an area a mile and a half downriver, and by then it was almost daylight. A little after four, Pakenham, hearing nothing, declared, "I will wait my own plans no longer."[5] Riding to inform Gibbs to continue the attack, he was stunned to hear even more bad news. "The forty-forth," reported Gibbs, "had not taken the fascines and ladders to the head of the column." With these two pieces of bad news Pakenham might have held off. Yet like Old Hickory, part of his success was his brashness. He himself would lead the attack. Riding to find the incompetent Mullens, he ordered him to get the fascines and ladders and convey them to the front. "Let me live till tomorrow and I'll hang him to the highest tree in that swamp," fumed Gibbs.[6] Pakenham then gave orders, in the words of one of his officers, "that the fatal, ever fatal rocket should be discharged as a signal to begin the assault on the left."[7]

British troops did not know what to make of this rocket. Visibility was less than two hundred yards. "A Congreve rocket was thrown up," wrote Captain John H. Cooke, "but whether from the enemy or not we could not tell; for some seconds it whizzed backwards and forwards in such a zig-zag way, that we all looked up to see whether it was coming down upon our heads."[8] Less than two minutes later, the British artillery roared to life. American artillery quickly followed. "Thus it was that the gunners of the English and the Americans were firing through the mist at random," continued Cooke. "And the first objects we saw, enclosed as we were in this little world of mist, were the cannon balls tearing up the ground and crossing one another, and bounding along like so many cricket balls through the air."[9]

Every American eye strained to see something through the mist. Lieutenant Spotts, from battery number six, was the first to discern a long red line advancing and began shelling the troops. Immediately the band of the Battalion D'Orleans began to play "Yankee Doodle." They played every military and patriotic song they knew during the course of the battle. The British advanced in rows, as many as nine deep. As a ball mowed down an oncoming redcoat, another moved to fill the ranks. "Stand to your guns," ordered Jackson as he rode up and down the line. "Don't waste your ammunition—see that every shot tells."

When the advancing red line was within two hundred yards, Jackson roared, "Give it to them boys; let us finish the business today." Carroll then gave the command: "Fire! Fire!"[10] The skilled riflemen had sighted their weapons to two hundred yards so that every shot would "tell." Two lines of Tennesseans and two lines of Kentuckians rotated so that a steady torrent of shells rained upon the approaching British. One line fired, then fell back to reload, while the next stepped up. The air was filled with the roar of cannon, the whistling of grapeshot, the screams of wounded and dying men, the whirring of chain-shot, and the whine of musketry. All the while redcoats dropped. One unknown Kentucky soldier described the scene: "Directly after the firing began, Capt. Patterson . . . an Irishman born, came running along." He then jumped upon the breastwork and shouted, "with a broad North of Ireland brogue, 'shoot low boys! Shoot low! Rake them—rake them! They're coming on their all fours.'"[11] The British fell in droves as Gibbs bravely led them on.

Confused and dazed by the enormous amount of lead filling the air, the British halted. "Where are the 44th?" cried the confused soldiers. "If we get to the ditch we have no means of scaling the lines!" "Here come the 44th! Here come the 44th," shouted a hopeful Gibbs. Led by Pakenham himself, the brave men rushed to the front, carrying the awaited fascines and ladders. A volley wounded Pakenham in the arm and killed his horse. Jumping onto another, he rallied the men to press on. Keane's reserve of nine hundred tartan-clad Highlanders was sent into the slaughter. Despite a withering fire that cut men down like a scythe, they formed a solid wall one hundred across and nine deep. They made it to one hundred yards of the American line. A round of grape caught Pakenham in the thigh, and a subsequent shot hit him in the groin. He died within minutes. Gibbs, too, was hit. He lingered hours in painful agony before expiring. Keane fell with a severe wound to the neck. Of the Highlanders, only 139 were left alive, and they turned for cover.[12] "We had run the gauntlet, from the left to the center in front of the American lines, under a cross fire," recounted Captain Cooke, "in hope of joining in the assault, and had a fine view of the sparkling of the musketry, and the liquid flashes from the cannon. . . . Regiments were shattered, broke, and dispersed—all order was at an end."[13] Even as General Lambert's reserve moved forward, he was met by the retreating men. As the only general not wounded, he took command. "As I advanced with the reserve," wrote Lambert, "at about two hundred and fifty yards from the line, I had the mortification to observe the whole falling back upon me in the greatest confusion."[14] Although the battle lasted more than two hours, in less than twenty-five minutes horrendous carnage had halted the oncoming assault.

Many sought refuge by hiding in ditches or behind trees and shrubs, but a score of soldiers managed to breach the American line. Major Wilkinson, along with Lieutenant Lavack and twenty others, struggled to cross the canal and climb the breastwork. As Wilkinson's head peered over the embankment, he was met with a hail of bullets. Impressed by his bravery, the Americans took his still breathing body to the rear. "Bear up my dear fellow," encouraged Major Smiley of the Kentucky reserve, "you are too brave a man to die." "I thank you from my heart," the dying man whispered. "It is all over with me. You can render me a favor; it is to communicate to my commander that I fell on your parapet, and died like a soldier and a true Englishman."[15] Lavack, with two bullet holes in his cap, leaped on the parapet and audaciously demanded the swords of two officers he quickly encountered. Surprised, the two looked at him, then behind him, and replied, "Oh, no; you are alone, therefore ought to consider yourself our prisoner." Months later, after being released at the conclusion of the war, Lavack recounted his tale. "Now, conceive my indignation," he told Cooke, "on looking round, to find that the two *leading regiments* had vanished, *as if the earth had opened and swallowed them up.*"[16]

There was one significant, if temporary, breach of the American line. Colonel Robert Rennie, upon seeing the rocket begin the battle, moved his troops rapidly along the river. As the outposts realized they were under attack, they fled and jumped into a redoubt (a dugout fortified position). Rennie's men quickly followed, climbed the walls, and also jumped into the enclosure. Hand-to-hand fighting followed. Noticing they were outnumbered, the Americans escaped the redoubt. Although wounded, Rennie jumped upon the wall. "Hurrah boys! The day is ours!" he cried. No sooner had the optimistic words come out of his mouth than a volley of rifle fire hit him and his companions. The remaining British fled as Patterson's guns from across the river and Captain Humphrey's battery poured grape into the British forces. As Rennie's body was examined, a heated discussion arose among the riflemen about whose bullet had killed him. "If he isn't hit above the eyebrows," remarked Withers, a merchant and crack marksman, "it wasn't my shot." Indeed the bullet hole was in the forehead just over the eyebrow. Withers therefore had the melancholy duty of sending the watch and other valuables to Rennie's widow, who was in the offshore fleet.[17]

The British also managed a victory on the west bank of the river. Although arriving later than expected and farther away than hoped, Thornton's men did land and move toward Morgan's position. Earlier in the evening Major Jean Arnaud and about two hundred militiamen went a mile down the river to report on any movement in that sector. For some reason, Arnaud allowed the men to sleep. The lone sentry's cry awoke the men as Thornton's men came upon them and nearly captured them. The Kentucky men, sent by Jackson at Morgan's request, joined the Louisianans and formed behind a sawmill race. After they exchanged fire, Morgan's aide feared they would soon be overrun and ordered a retreat. The result was panic. Although Morgan tried to hold the line, even chasing the men on horseback, it was a rout. Fearing his guns would be captured, Patterson ordered them spiked and ammunition thrown into the river. He then escaped. Thornton's men did capture the guns and desperately tried to repair them. Just as he had completed this task, he was ordered to retreat because the battle was over.[18]

During the course of the battle, Jackson calmly watched the progress from a rise near the center. He allowed his officers to do their duty, and they succeeded. When it was obvious that the battle was winding down, Major Hinds, whose relief column was fresh, pressed the general to let him follow and attack the fleeing redcoats. Uncharacteristically Jackson refused the request. "I felt a confidence that the safety of the city was most probably assured," he said later, giving a reason for the decision, "and hence that nothing calculated to reverse the good fortune we had met should be attempted."[19] At eight o'clock Jackson ordered the small arms firing to cease. Walking along his front, he congratulated and spoke encouraging words to his men, telling them how proud he was to command them. The band struck up "Hail Columbia," and the men cheered as Jackson moved along the line. Soon the cannons also ceased. Slowly as the smoke from the guns dispersed, and as the extent of the British devastation became apparent, even the cheering ceased.

"I never had so grand and awful an idea of the resurrection as on that day," recalled Old Hickory later. "I saw in the distance more than five hundred Britons emerging from the heaps of their dead comrades, all over the plain, rising up, and still more distinctly visible as the field became clearer, coming forward and surrendering as prisoners of war to our soldiers."[20] For two hundred yards in front of Carroll's position the ground was literally covered by the dead. So thick were they upon the ground, Walker recounted, "From the American ditch you could have walked a quarter of a mile to the front on the bodies of the killed and disabled." The effect of the cannon was so accurate that "they fell in their tracks; in some places, whole platoons lay together, as if killed by the same discharge."[21] From all over the field, the painful melancholy cries of the wounded for aid and water filled the air. "Some lying quite dead, others mortally wounded, pitching and tumbling about in the agonies of death," wrote one eyewitness. "Some had their heads shot off, some their legs, some their arms. Some were laughing, some crying, some groaning, and some screaming. There was every variety of sight and sound."[22] The Americans stood in awestruck silence as they saw what their weapons had done.

The final tally for the American casualties on January 8 was 13 killed, 39 wounded, and 19 missing.[23] For the British losses, Lambert reported, "Our loss has been very severe, but I trust it will not be considered, notwithstanding the failure, that this army has suffered the military character to be tarnished." He suffered 291 killed, 1,262 wounded, and 484 missing or captured.[24] As was the custom of the day for transporting famous personages, like Admiral Nelson, back to England for burial, Pakenham and Gibbs were disemboweled and their remains placed in casks of rum for preservation. In his letter to Monroe, Jackson initially thought the number might be 1,500 for British casualties, but later Inspector General Haynes put the total at 2,600. The general realized that the inequity of the numbers might be questioned and that they might not "everywhere be fully credited; Yet I am perfectly satisfied that the amount is not exaggerated on the one part, nor underated on the other."[25]

Even without permission, many Americans moved among the wounded, providing water and aid. Many also went among the dead, stripping them of valuables and souvenirs later to be sold in New Orleans. They brought many behind their lines to provide emergency aid. On the same day, January 8, Lambert praised the kind, humane treatment of his wounded; he also requested the return of his captured officers and permission for an unarmed party to bury the dead and collect the wounded.[26] Jackson agreed to the terms and then set a ceasefire until the next day at noon.[27] For the next few days soldiers buried their dead comrades in mass shallow graves. Weeks later, rains that overflowed the river caused arms and legs to stick out of the ground. Even a year later the odor of rotting flesh filled the air in New Orleans, causing fear that disease might break out. Forty years later the field was covered with stunted cypress trees.[28]

After receiving a report that the British were digging redoubts and might be preparing for another battle, the general expressed his desire to press the attack. "What do you want more," asked his aide Edward Livingston, "your object is gained—the city is saved—the British have retired."[29] Livingston was right. Unbeknownst to Jackson, the redcoats were preparing to leave. At nine in the evening of the eighteenth, they began to march through swamps and marshes. Soon they were into muck up to their knees, and one officer went up to his neck in quicksand. Another enemy threatened the retreat. "Just before dark I saw an *alligator* emerge from the water and penetrate the wilderness of reeds which encircled us . . . to look out for the enemy was a secondary consideration," reported a British soldier, "The word was, look out for the *alligators*."[30] On January 18, the British sailed away, leaving eighty seriously wounded as well as fourteen cannon and three thousand cannonballs, among other property.[31]

On January 27, 1815, Jackson wrote to his friend Governor Blount: "The unerring hand of Providence shielded my men from the showers of bombs, balls and rockets; when, on the other hand, it appeared that every ball and bomb from our lines was charged with the mission of death." The British forces in that part of the country were broken; they lost officers and "the flower of their army." Jackson believed the battle would bring about the peace sought in Ghent (he still did not know of the treaty). Despite his victory, he added, "Three thousand stand of arms more than I had on the 8th, in my opinion, have placed the whole British army in my hands. But the Lord's will be done."[32] Little did the general know that the news of his victory would soon spread over the country and make him the hero of New Orleans and a presidential contender.

The boost in morale to the national spirit brought by the victory in New Orleans cannot be overstated. As 1815 dawned, the United States capital had been invaded and burned; Congress was disunited and ineffective; Federalists convened in Hartford, Connecticut; and talk of New England's support for the British and even secession from the Union filled the press. An unusually violent snowstorm, lasting three days, hit the Northeast, making news difficult to get through; the war was going badly in the North; and news that the British sent a huge force to invade New Orleans traveled around the country. All of this made for an atmosphere of foreboding. America was fighting a second time for its right to be independent—free from European interference—and things were not going well. Rumors of defeat along the Gulf Coast sprang up as inconclusive reports from the front dribbled in.

CHAPTER FIFTEEN

The Hero of New Orleans

"Glory be to God that the barbarians have been defeated.
Glory to Jackson. . . . Glory to the militia."

—Headlines in *Niles' Weekly Register*, February 14, 1815

THE DAY AFTER the great battle, the city of New Orleans
began what would become a national period of celebration.
Upon watching the British sails vanish, Jackson wrote the Abbe
Duborg, apostolic minister of the diocese of Louisiana and the
Floridas asking for a special religious observance to celebrate
the recent victory. "The signal interposition of heaven," he
began in his letter to the Abbe, "in giving success to our arms
against the Enemy, who: so lately landed on our Shores. . . .
Permit me therefore to entreat that you will cause the service of
public thanksgiving to be performed in the Cathedral in token
at once of the great assistance we have recd. From the *ruler of*

all Events and of our humble sense of it."[1] Duborg immediately agreed to the idea and suggested Tuesday, January 23, as a date for the event. "I will make the dispositions for the ceremony," he replied, "the brightest ornament of which will be *yourself*, General, surrounded by your brave army."[2] On January 20, 1815, the victorious general entered the city of New Orleans, the first time since December 23. Enthusiastic, grateful, and cheering crowds greeted him.

As in previous campaigns, Jackson praised the bravery of his men and credited them with the victory. "The enemy has retreated," he addressed the assembled troops, "and your general now has leisure to proclaim to the world what he has noticed with admiration and pride—your undaunted courage, your patriotism and patience under hardships and fatigues." No wonder the men loved him. He shared their suffering as well as the glory for his victories. He also gave thanks to God. "Let us be grateful to the God of battles," he continued, "who has directed the arrows of indignation against our invaders, while he covered with his protecting shield the brave defenders of their country." He then praised each individual unit and its commander.[3]

The news of Jackson's victory hit Washington on February 4, 1815, like a jolt of electricity. The city and the nation went wild with excitement—finally, some good news. With the largest type it had, the *National Intelligencer* blared its headlines: "ALMOST INCREDIBLE VICTORY!!!" *Niles' Weekly Register* proclaimed, "Glory be to God that the barbarians have been defeated. Glory to Jackson. . . . Glory to the militia. Sons of freedom . . . benefactors of your country . . . all hail."[4]

Philadelphia declared "a general illumination" of the city, and despite the snow, revelers packed the streets. One resident placed a transparency in his window depicting the general on horseback in pursuit of the enemy, and it bore the motto, "This day shall ne'er go by from this day to the ending of the world, but He [Jackson], in it shall be remembered."[5] Northerners who had never heard the name of Andrew Jackson began to ask who he was and where he came from. From such questions are legends made, as answers were not always verified. Yet even better news was on the way.

On February 13, the air was filled with the sounds of "Peace! Peace!" as news reached Washington that both sides had signed the peace treaty in Ghent. After ratification, the treaty would go into effect, bringing an end to the War of 1812. Half an hour after the news reached New York, "Broadway was one living sea of shouting, rejoicing people . . . tens of thousands of people were marching about with candles, lamps and torches—making the jubilant street appear like a gay and gorgeous procession."[6] Similar scenes occurred around the nation.

The victory at New Orleans boosted both the domestic national spirit and the respect for the young nation abroad. America had once again affirmed its independence from England and could now take its rightful place among the major nations of the world. For the first time, America had won a decisive victory over a European country without the aid of another European country. Military might impressed the European powers. America gained new respect as it, too, possessed the power not only to raise an army but also to defeat the nation that had ruled the waves for centuries and only recently sent Napoleon into exile.

The effect at home was even more profound. The entire country had a new sense of pride and nationalism. The sectionalism evidenced by the Federalist discontent in New England evaporated. Facing and defeating a common enemy allowed a stronger sense of belonging to a nation—and not just a state—to emerge. "From that time on," wrote William Graham Sumner, "the Union had less of the character of a temporary experiment. The country had also won respect abroad, and was recognized in the family of nations as it never been before."[7] No one was more associated with the victory that sparked this newfound nationalism and pride than the hero of New Orleans—as he would henceforth be known—General Andrew Jackson.

Jackson became the face of the victory over the British. The public viewed the federal government as being unequal to the task of defeating the enemy. Madison himself would praise Jackson's actions as a way to focus attention away from the failures of his administration.[8] Nearly every state in the Union as well as the federal government passed resolutions praising the general and his men. Congress authorized a gold medal to be struck in his honor. It was Jackson who had defeated the British—and done so convincingly. Due to this victory, Old Hickory would forever take his place in the pantheon of American heroes. "Jackson had been the soul of the defence from the beginning," concluded Sumner, "and to his energy and perseverance success was due."[9] Perhaps the "Great Compromiser" and future Speaker of the House from Kentucky, Henry Clay, encapsulated the pride now felt by many Americans. After hearing of the treaty while in Paris, he remarked, "*Now*, I can go to England without mortification."[10]

Although he had heard from Livingston, who was aboard a British ship arranging for prisoner transfer and arrived back in the city on February 19, that the treaty had been signed, Jackson cautiously refused to recognize the peace until he received official word from Washington of its ratification. "I believe you will not think me too sanguine in the belief that Louisiana is now clear of its enemy," he had written Monroe on January 19, and nothing that had happened since caused him to change his mind.[11] Like any good general, he continued to make preparations for a counterattack. His militia remained on duty, and martial law continued. That did not sit well with the French Creoles who wanted to go home. Many began to leave their posts. Public sentiment began to turn against the victorious general.

Two days after Livingston's news was made public, an article appeared in the *Louisiana Gazette* in essence confirming the rumor that peace had been proclaimed. Jackson responded that he had no official word and that no changes would occur until he had. A few days later, a state legislator, Mr. Louaillier, wrote a scathing letter to the editor demanding an end to martial law—in effect defying Jackson. The general responded by arresting Louaillier. His attorney then went to US district judge Dominick A. Hall requesting and receiving a writ of habeas corpus. When Jackson heard of this, he promptly issued an order. "Having recd information that Dominick A. Hall has been engaged in a[i]ding abetting and exciting mutiny in my camp," he angrily wrote, "you will forthwith . . . arrest and [confine] him."[12] He had the district judge arrested! On March 13 official word reached Jackson of the ratification of the treaty. He ended martial law, Louaillier and the judge went free—but that was not the end of Jackson's problems.

On March 31, Jackson appeared in court to answer for his high-handed actions. As soon as he arrived and was recognized— he was wearing civilian clothes—the crowd erupted with shouts of praise. Fearing a hostile mob, the judge ordered adjournment. Jackson then arose and, standing straight, addressed the court and the people: "There is no danger here; there shall be none—the same arm that protected from outrage this city . . . will shield and protect this court, or perish in the effort."[13] Jackson knew how to turn a phrase and how to appeal to the masses. He was fined one thousand dollars, which he personally paid, not accepting contributions from others. He was carried out of the courtroom on the shoulders of his admirers. He spent the next few weeks in the Crescent City settling accounts, resting, and receiving the accolades of well-wishers. His journey home was marked by celebrations and the cheers of crowds. On May 15 he, Rachel, and their adopted son, Andrew, who had joined him in New Orleans, arrived back in Nashville.

A tremendous crowd welcomed him home. Representative Felix Grundy gave a speech extolling his virtues and those of his brave troops—many of whom were in the crowd. "Sir; I am at a loss to express my feelings," responded the general. "The approbation of my fellow-citizens is to me the richest reward. Through you, sir," he addressed Grundy, "I beg leave to assure them that I am *this* day amply compensated for every toil and labor."[14] Of course the crowd loved his humility, brevity, and heartfelt emotion. The celebrations continued as he gave several speeches to groups honoring him.

He spent the rest of the summer recuperating and resting. The bullets in his chest and arm still plagued him, as did his intestinal problems. In October he was rested enough to make the triumphal sojourn to Washington, DC. In Lynchburg a tumultuous welcome was followed by a lavish feast. Among the guests was perhaps the most respected man in America at the time—seventy-two-year-old Thomas Jefferson. "Honor and gratitude," toasted the former president, "to those who have filled the measure of their country's honor."[15] Jackson responded with a toast to Jefferson and the future president James Monroe.

Within a space of sixteen months, Jackson had gone from being an obscure southern planter to one of the most recognized and admired persons in the country. His name, like that of Washington before him and others to come after him, was on the lips of all because of his military successes. Would he parlay this popularity into political office? "[There is] but little doubt," wrote Colonel Andrew Hymes, who had access to the sentiments of high-ranking political and military figures, "with the proper management of your friends, that you might be elevated to the highest Office in the American Government."[16] Heady stuff for a poor southern boy, orphaned before the age of fifteen and not born into the aristocratic class of those presidents who preceded him. Yet he was not yet finished with his military career.

CHAPTER SIXTEEN

The Indian Question

"The [white] inhabitants of Territories are Citizens of the
United States and entitled to all the rights thereof, the
Indians are Subjects and entitled to their protection and
fostering care."

—Jackson's views on Indian citizenship

AT THE CONCLUSION of the War of 1812 the army was
reduced to ten thousand men and divided into two geographi-
cal divisions, each commanded by a major general. Jacob Brown
was to command the northern region, and Jackson the southern,
which included most of the then Northwest, with pay of $2,400
per year plus $1,652 for expenses. The Hermitage became his
headquarters. His primary duty was to sort out all the land disputes with the tribes in the South and keep an eye on the porous
border with Spanish Florida where remnants of the Red Sticks

and hostile Seminoles, egged on by a rogue ex-Royal Marine, Edward Nicholls, exchanged atrocities with frontier settlers. Finding a solution to these two problems would again thrust the general into the national spotlight and cause a war with international ramifications.

The Treaty of Ghent, which ended the War of 1812, contained a proviso that was sure to cause trouble along the southern frontier. Article IX ordered the United States to restore all lands possessed by the Indians in 1811. In effect, this provision nullified the Treaty of Fort Jackson and returned nearly twenty-three million acres to the Creeks. Moreover, the new secretary of war, William H. Crawford, agreed to return an additional four million acres of land to the Cherokees, who disputed possession with the Creeks. A furious Jackson would have none of it. His reply to Crawford emphasized two points: he had no knowledge of any agreement between the Cherokees and Creeks over the disputed area; and if there was an agreement as a matter of principle of right and justice, the surrender ought never to have been made in the first place. The rest of the letter outlined the complexities of defining all the boundaries and the impossibility of carrying out such an order. At present all the disputed land was in the process of being settled by whites. "I have now done; political discussion is not the province of a military officer," he concluded. "As a man, I am entitled to my opinion, and have given it freely."[1]

This was classic Jackson. We may disagree with his policies, but we must at least grant that he was consistent. He kept his eye on the overall strategic expansionist goal of the nation. In his mind the United States needed to secure and control the entire

Gulf Coast and both East and West Florida (West Florida contained the lower sections of Alabama and Mississippi. The US would virtually control this area after 1812) to prevent a future attack from that area and to open the area for settlement. Cuba would soon be added to this list of desired national acquisitions. This had always been his main objective. The British continued to stir up and arm the hostile Indians, and the weak and crumbling Spanish Empire was incapable of stopping them. Even now a so-called Negro fort, located along the Apalachicola River, provided refuge for runaway slaves from neighboring states, and the Spanish did nothing. Our national borders were both unclear and insecure. Within these borders, Indians, who were not subject to either state or federal law, controlled huge chunks of land, preventing settlement. This, too, caused insecurity. Therefore an issue of national security existed on both fronts, and he would do something about it, even if it meant disregarding—or at least ignoring—orders. Indeed, the blurring of the lines between his actions as a "military officer" and his opinions as a "man" often occurred.

On March 4, 1817, the date of James Monroe's inauguration (the first president to be sworn in outdoors), Jackson wrote him a letter outlining his objectives in the area. This letter provides us with keen insight into his beliefs and goals in dealing with the Indians. As immoral or unfair as we might view his actions today, he was guided by what he thought best for the nation. Jackson spelled out his views concerning how the federal government ought to deal with both the foreign threat and the Indians. The nation's first priority was to remedy the "defenceless situation of

New Orleans, Mobile and their dependencies, in consequence of the want of repairs to the old Fortifications and the erection of others which are absolutely necessary for their safety." Next he recommended a "permanent settlement of all Lands acquired from the Creek Indians." If these two actions were taken, "Louisiana may be considered safe, and the lower Country impregnable to an enemy."[2]

As a further action, the Chickasaw land on the Ohio River in Kentucky and on the east bank of the Mississippi should be obtained and open to settlement. The effect would be to cut off contact with the northern and southern tribes—clearly he feared another Tecumseh—and to ensure control of traffic on both rivers. How should this land be acquired?

"I have long viewed treaties with the Indians an absurdity not to be reconciled to the principles of our government," he continued. "The Indians are the subjects of the United States, inhabiting its territory and acknowledging its sovereignty, then is it not absurd for the sovereign to negotiate by treaty with the subjects." According to Jackson, Congress had the right to regulate all Indian affairs, just as it did the territories. It could do with the Indians and their land as it willed. He envisioned a two-tiered class system. The difference was, "the inhabitants of Territories are Citizens of the United States and entitled to all the rights thereof, the Indians are Subjects and entitled to their protection and fostering care." Indians had "possessory rights" or the ability to hunt and fish on the lands while citizens had "the right of soil or Domain."[3] The tribes should not be considered sovereign nations—which was the federal policy—but subjects under control of the legislature. Indians could use the land, but as long as they practiced their traditional lifestyle, they could not own it.

"Their existence and happiness now depend upon a change in their habits and customs," opined the general. "The game being destroyed they can no longer exist by their bows and arrows and Gun." These must be laid aside, and they must now "produce by labour; from the earth a subsitance; in short they must be civilized."[4] This would not happen if they were allowed to roam over vast areas of land. If forced to live on smaller parcels of land, they would become farmers and therefore "civilized." By allowing the present circumstances to continue, the federal government actually did an injustice to the Indians. Treaties had been consistently violated and broken; chiefs received bribes to enrich themselves; but the average Indians saw only poverty and degradation and had no say in their own governance. Individual land ownership would remedy this abuse.[5]

As previously noted, the concept of Indian removal was not new. Jefferson suggested it in 1803, and the Louisiana Purchase seemed allow for this to happen. Governor Willie Blount wrote about it to Jackson as early as December 1809. "It would be in the interest of the United States," he wrote, "to accede to the proposal of this State respecting an exchange of territory with the Cherokees and Chickasaws . . . to give them lands west of the Mississippi in exchange for their claim." It would be to their advantage to do so as there they could "preserve their national character" more easily than in the midst of encroaching white settlers. Clearly Jackson agreed with this position.[6]

Soon after writing this letter, Jackson received authorization to "extinguish the Indian titles" concluded in 1806 with the Cherokees.[7] In 1808, this nation had agreed to exchange lands east of the Mississippi for lands in Arkansas. In fact many Cherokees had already moved into this area but failed to cede the corresponding land in the East. Old Hickory was to rectify this and even offer more land for trade. He thus received authorization to implement the plan he had always advocated—the removal of the Indians from east of the Mississippi and their relocation on the west side. In Jackson's experience the cultures of the sedentary agricultural whites and the free-roaming Indians were incompatible. Warfare and bloodshed resulted. Without separation the Indian lifestyle, and indeed their very existence, was in jeopardy. The exchange of land was both necessary and honorable. Of course should the Indians fail to find it so, they would face the full wrath of Sharp Knife and his army. They literally had no choice but to accept.

By the end of 1818, treaties with the Cherokees, Choctaws, and Chickasaws had divested them of most of their land in the East and established the concept of Indian removal. The Choctaws and Chickasaws agreed to removal, but due to government inefficiency, the process did not begin until late fall, resulting in many avoidable casualties. This system of callous governmental abuse and poor timing would later result in the even more catastrophic removal of the Cherokees under then President Jackson and will be dealt with in a later chapter.[8]

With the domestic threat settled for the time being with the treaties of 1818, the general could now focus on the international

THE INDIAN QUESTION ★ 173

threat of the Spanish in East Florida. What he needed was a reason, an incident, any impropriety, to give him the excuse to invade and take Florida. A haven for escaped slaves gave him that opportunity.

CHAPTER SEVENTEEN

The First Seminole War

"The protection of our citizens will require that the Wolf be struck in his den."

—Jackson's rationale for invading Florida

FOR DECADES SPANISH Florida had been a safe haven for runaway slaves and a home to free blacks. Although the Seminoles occasionally captured the runaways and sold them back into captivity, for the most part they coexisted. As mentioned earlier, the rogue English Marine, Edward Nicholls, had both assisted and encouraged the Red Sticks and the Seminoles in their roles as allies to the British during the war. He had built a well-constructed fort along the Apalachicola River, sixty miles below the Georgia line, around which hundreds of blacks had built farms. When Nicholls departed for England in the summer of 1815, never to be seen in America again, he left the fort

well armed with cannon, small arms, and powder. The freed-
men took over the fort, essentially controlling traffic on the river
from the Gulf to Fort Scott in Georgia. This became known as
the Negro fort and was a great source of irritation to slavehold-
ers. The Spanish authorities, located more than one hundred
miles west, were powerless to control the situation. In response
to appeals, the slave-owning Jackson decided to act.

On April 23, 1816, he wrote a letter to the Spanish commandant, Mauricio de Zuniga. He informed the commandant
that he was authorized by his government to "make known to
you that a negro fort erected during our late war with Britain . . .
has been strengthened . . . and is now occupied by upwards of
two-hundred and fifty negroes many of whom have been enticed
away from the service of their masters . . . all of whom are well
clothed and disciplined." If the Spanish government did not
immediately give orders to dispel this "Banditti," the action
would "compel us in self Defence to destroy them."[1] With this
letter, carried to Pensacola by Captain Amelung, Jackson laid the
groundwork for an invasion of Florida.

The commandant replied with a ten-page letter. He had
written his commander in Havana for permission to destroy the
fort but had not yet received a reply. He hoped Jackson would
do nothing to violate Spanish authority. A few months later,
however, regular army General George Pendleton Gaines (who
constructed Fort Scott) sent a force to confront the fort. Needing
to fire only one well-placed cannon ball, heated red hot by a furnace, a gunner hit the powder magazine and blew the Negro fort
into oblivion. Only 3 of the 354 inhabitants escaped the blast.[2]

The destruction of the fort did not end the border disputes, however. Of more enduring concern were the Seminoles and Creeks who crossed the border and raided Georgia only to escape back into Florida. On April 2, 1817, Jackson received word from Gaines of a fresh outrage. "A party of Indians attacked a defenceless family and massacred a woman (Mrs. Garrot) and her two children," he explained, "the woman and eldest child were scalped, the house robbed and set on fire."[3] The perpetrators then escaped into Spanish Florida. With this letter, Gaines included a letter signed by Alexander Arbuthnot, whom Gaines characterized as one of those *"self-styled Philanthropists"* who have acted as "British Agents—fomenting a spirit of discord."[4] Three months later, Gaines again informed Jackson of Arbuthnot's activities, labeling him as the "prime director" of Seminole affairs.[5] The hero of New Orleans would soon deal with him.

Neamathla was a feisty Seminole chief who presided over a small settlement, known as Fowltown, consisting of Seminoles, Red Sticks, and runaway slaves. A red pole (symbol of the Red Sticks) was raised in the center of the town. Located just north of the Florida border, on ground he insisted was ceded by the US government, it became a focal point for Indian resistance. Neamathala had written a letter to the commander at Fort Scott, Colonel Twiggs, that if he as much as "cut a stick of wood on the east side of the Flint [River]," he would defend it. When Gaines arrived at the fort, he sent Twiggs and a force of 250 men to bring in Neamathala for questioning. "In the event of resistance," ordered Gaines, he was "to treat them as enemies."[6]

When they saw the approaching troops, the Indians defended themselves, but soon escaped into the woods. Before setting fire to the town, Twiggs discovered a British uniform and a certificate that Neamathala had been a faithful friend of the British. The destruction of Fowltown began the First Seminole War.[7]

The Seminoles were quick to respond. "It is my duty to report to you an affair of a more serious and disastrous character than has heretofore occurred upon this frontier," wrote Gaines to Jackson on December 2, 1817. "A large party of Seminola Indians" along the Apalachicola River ambushed a boat carrying forty soldiers and seven wives and killed all but six soldiers, who escaped, and a woman, who was taken hostage. One escapee reported the number of hostiles as at least five hundred.[8] Parton provides additional information that there were also four children who were grabbed by the heels and had their heads smashed against the sides of the boat and that both men and women were scalped.[9]

Upon hearing this news, Jackson responded by writing to John C. Calhoun, the newly appointed secretary of war. "The protection of our citizens," he counseled, "will require that the Wolf be struck in his den; for, rest assured, if ever the Indians find out that the territorial boundary of Spain is to be a sanctuary, their murders will be multiplied."[10] He reminded Calhoun of Spain's duty and subsequent inability to control the Indians within its borders. Since the Spanish were apparently not fulfilling this obligation, "necessity will justify the measure . . . to follow the marauders, and punish them in their retreat."[11] Jackson now had his excuse to invade, and he exploited it to the fullest.

Undoubtedly Old Hickory was elated at the response. On December 26, Calhoun ordered him to Fort Scott to take command. Calhoun had previously ordered Gaines to "penetrate to the Seminole Towns, through the Floridas." Therefore Jackson was to continue with these orders and "adopt the necessary measures to terminate a conflict" that, although unwanted, had begun.[12] Jackson could scarcely contain his excitement at being given orders to pursue the hostiles "through the Floridas." The ensuing controversial actions of Old Hickory embroiled the United States in a confrontation with Spain that resulted in the acquisition of Florida.

Even more to his liking must have been the letter he received from Monroe himself, dated December, 28, 1817. The president reiterated Calhoun's missive. The Indians have "long violated our rights & insulted our national character. The mov'ment will bring you, on a theatre, when possibly you may have other services to perform." He concluded by stating, "This is not a time for you to think of repose [Jackson was considering retirement at the time]. Great interests are at issue, and until our course is carried through triumphantly & every species of danger to which it is exposed is settled on the most solid foundation, you ought not to withdraw your active support from it."[13] Remini believes this letter implicitly gave Jackson the green light to seize Florida.

On January 6, Jackson wrote President Monroe a confidential letter expressing his approval of the orders from Calhoun and proposing to carry them a step forward. Gaines's orders "to enter the Territory of Spain and chastise the Ruthless Savages . . . will meet, not only the approbation of your country but the approbation of Heaven." Since Gaines had already taken Amelia Island, he suggested it would be appropriate to "simultaneously" seize the whole of East Florida and hold it "as an indemnity for the outrages of Spain upon the property of our Citizens." By the acquisition of Florida, he could spare the United States a war with Spain allied with another European power: "This [the taking of East Florida] can be done without implicating the Government." He continued, "Let it be signified to me through any channel, (say, Mr. J. Rhea) [the representative from Tennessee] that the possession of the Floridas would be desirable to the United States, and in sixty days it will be accomplished."[14] In effect, Jackson wanted executive authority to begin a war with Spain. Subsequent letters provided him the rationalization to fulfill his longtime goal of ending European presence in the Southeast.

No reply has been found to this letter. On January 30, Monroe directed Calhoun to instruct Jackson "not to attack any post occupied by Spanish troops, from the possibility, that it might bring the allied powers on us."[15] In view of subsequent events, a crucial question arises. Why did Monroe order Calhoun to write Jackson and not do it himself since Jackson had confidentially written to the president? There is also no record of Calhoun issuing any orders to Old Hickory. There are several possible reponses: Monroe did not actually direct Calhoun to give these orders, the secretary disobeyed an order from the president, or both complicitly agreed with the general's actions but did not want to be blamed if the incursion blew up in their faces. Historians David S. and Jeanne T. Heidler propose another option. "Jackson was lying," they concluded, because "not until 1827 [Jackson was then a presidential candidate] did Jackson say he received the Rhea letter giving Monroe's permission to attack the Spanish posts."[16] Monroe would later claim that he was sick when he received Jackson's letter of January 6, that he did not read it until after the Florida incursion, and that he had never spoken with Rhea.[17] Rhea, however, sent a letter to Jackson, dated January 12, 1818. "I expected you would receive the letter you allude to," wrote the congressman, "and it gives me pleasure to know you have it. . . . You see by it the sentiments of the President respecting you are the same." Furthermore he was glad that "the plan of the President is satisfactory to you."[18] In any case the hero felt justified and continued his actions.

Jackson immediately contacted Coffee. "If I can get 1200 mounted gunmen from Tennessee with my regular force," he believed, he could "drive into the Gulf all the Indians and their adherents by them."[19] On January 22, 1818, he departed the Hermitage for Fort Scott. As he passed through Tennessee, as he suspected, "volunteers were flocking to the standard of their country," and the only problem he faced, again, was the lack of adequate weapons.[20] Lack of food, bad weather, and swollen streams also plagued his journey and he was forced to continue with only the Georgia militia and a few regulars. On March 9, the starving, tired, and wet troops arrived at Fort Scott. Despite the trials, he arrived with "the troops in good health," he wrote Rachel on March 26, "not having lost one man by sickness or any other casualty." He was sad that the "Volunteers from Tennessee" had not yet arrived, but he had left supplies for them along the way.[21] Finding no supplies at the fort, he determined to march as soon as feasible to meet the supply boats. On March 12, he again crossed into Spanish Florida. The invasion had begun.

For once something good happened. A day later they encountered a supply boat on the Apalachicola River commanded by US Navy Captain Isaac McKeever. The men ate until they were full for the first time in weeks. On March 16, the troops arrived at the remains of the Negro fort. Approving of the overall strategic location of the fort, Jackson set Lieutenant James Gadsden the task of rebuilding the fort. Old Hickory approved of this plan and renamed it Fort Gadsden.[22] For ten days the troops rested and ate.

On March 26, they headed northeast toward Saint Marks. Five days later the Volunteers and friendly Creeks joined them. The general shared his intelligence with Captain McKeever that "Francis, or Hillis Hago, and Peter McQueen, prophets, who excited the Red Sticks in their late war against the United States, and are now exciting the Seminoles to similar acts of hostility, are at or in the neighborhood of St. Marks." Furthermore they had been joined by the British George Woodbine and Arbuthnot and runaway slaves. Jackson believed "these men should be captured and made examples of." He instructed McKeever to patrol the coastal areas and capture these men should they try to escape.[23] Robert Ambrister, also a British subject, would join Arbuthnot. Unlike Arbuthnot, however, he counseled the Indians to war, and he was less concerned about Indian welfare than his own. Both men would soon meet their nemesis.

As the general approached Saint Marks, his advance guard

of spies encountered a group of Indians who gave a "spirited attack" for a brief period before they fled. Cautiously Jackson pursued through the Mekasukian towns and the next day burned more than three hundred homes. (The Miccosukee were part of the Seminole nation.) He found a large supply of corn and cattle as well as "more than fifty fresh scalps." In the center of the town was "the old red stick's standard, *A red Pole*, was erected, crowned with scalps." Moreover, he believed the Spanish at that fort had aided and abetted the Seminoles. "These considerations," he continued in a letter to Calhoun, "determined me to occupy it [Saint Marks] with an American force."[24] Jackson believed the hostiles were headed for Saint Marks, and he was hot on their trail.

Upon arrival at that town, Jackson sent a letter to the commandant of the fort, Don Francisco Caso y Luengo. "To chastise a Savage foe," explained Jackson to the commandant on April 6, 1818, "compelled The President to direct me to march my army into Florida."[25] He then recounted his experiences in the Mekasuka town and how he had received intelligence that these enemies had "obtained their supply of ammunition from St. Marks." Therefore, "I deem it expedient to garrison that fortress with American Troops until the close of the present war." Since these hostiles had also acted against the king of Spain, "I came not as an Enemy but as the Friend of Spain."[26] This letter is another example of classic Jackson reasoning, manipulation, and bending others to his will. Knowing that ultimately his goal was to get the Spanish out of Florida, he made it sound like they were allies against the Indians. How could Luengo refuse such an offer from the more powerful army? Still, he wanted "time to reflect" on the offer.

The impatient general was not one to wait, and he ordered Major Twiggs to advance into the fort. There was no opposition as the Spanish flag was hauled down, and he gave the order to "hoist the Stars Spangled banner on the ramparts of Fort St. Marks."[27] Upon inspection of the fort, Jackson found clear evidence the Spanish had aided the hostiles. In addition he found and imprisoned the aged Arbuthnot, holding him for trial. At almost the same time, Captain McKeever, while patrolling the river, captured two Creek chieftains, Josiah Francis (aka Hillis Hadjo) and Himollemico. Jackson ordered both hung on April 8, and gave them decent burials.

Hearing that a large force of Seminoles was located about a hundred miles east along the Suwannee River, in an area known as the Bowlegs Towns, the general set off on April 9 with eight days' supply of food for his nearly 5,000 man force of regulars, volunteers, and Indian allies. Jackson believed Chief Bowlegs was the leader of a large force of runaway slaves and Seminoles. Surely the destruction of his principal town would end the Indian resistance in Florida. When he reached the town on April 16, he immediately attacked and burned more than three hundred dwellings. Having been warned, the inhabitants had fled.

A couple of nights later, the other English conspirator, Robert Ambrister, stumbled into the town, unaware that Jackson possessed it. He was captured and searched. On his person was a note from Arbuthnot warning his son that Jackson was coming and he should flee. The general knew exactly what he wanted to do with both men. "I hope the execution of these two unprincipled villains," he reported to Secretary Calhoun, "will prove an awful example to the world."[28] He then returned to Saint Marks and tried and executed both men on April 29, 1818.[29]

"The hand of heaven has been pointed against the exciters of this war," he assured Rachel on April 20, 1818, "every principal villain has been either killed or taken. . . . I think I may say that the Indian war is at an end for the present, the enemy is scattered over the whole face of the Earth, and least one half must starve and die of disease."[30] There remained only the capture of the Spanish capital at Pensacola to complete his mission.

In a letter to Calhoun, May 5, 1818, Jackson justified his proceeding to Pensacola and possible occupation of that city. "It has been stated," began the general, "that the Indians at war with the U States have free access into Pensacola." These beliefs "compell me to make a movement to the West."[31] If he was correct, Pensacola must be occupied with an "American force." He trusted the actions he must take would " meet with the approbation of the President," since they were "adopted in pursuance of your instructions."[32]

On May 24, Jackson arrived at Pensacola. The day before, Governor Jose Masot wrote Jackson and protested his presence as "an insult offered to his King and Master." If the general continued, Masot warned that he would repulse Jackson "force to force," which would result in "an effusion of blood."[33] In reply, Jackson outlined what had brought him to this city: "This is the third time that American Troops have been compelled to enter Pensaco[la] from the same causes."[34] He further justified his actions on the "principle of self defence." If Masot did not surrender, "I shall enter Pensacola by violence and assume the Government." He concluded the letter by calling Masot "the aggressor and the blood which may be shed . . . will rest on your head."[35]

In the face of the American forces, Masot retreated to Fort Barrancas and left Luis Piernas in command of the town. Jackson heard that Piernas was prepared to fire on his troops, and he responded, "If such orders are carried into effect, I will put to death every man found in arms."[36] He next warned Masot to give up the fort: firing on the Americans must "draw upon you the vengeance of an irritated Soldiery."[37] Despite these warnings, Masot refused. The general brought forth cannon, which fired at the fort until Masot surrendered at 3:00 p.m on May 27.

An exhausted Jackson informed President Monroe on June 2, 1818, that the war was over. America now controlled Florida with the exception of the fort at Saint Augustine. With typical Jackson bravado he told the president if he could have a few more guns, "he would insure Ft St Augustine add another Regt. And one Frigate and I will insure Cuba in a few days."[38] The old soldier, however, was spitting blood, had a bad cough, and was nothing but skin and bones. Yet, he assured Rachel, he was "still able to march on foot 25 miles a day."[39] He was returning to Nashville and would see his beloved Rachel on June 25 if all went well.

In less than three months, Old Hickory had violated the sovereignty of Spain, taking over one of its forts and destroying its main garrison in Pensacola, established a provisional government in what technically was Spanish territory, broken the back of Seminole resistance, and executed two British subjects. The last outrage caused parliamentary debate and protests in the streets of London against the US government and especially Jackson, who was referred to as a "tyrant, ruffian and murderer" in the press. Although hotheads argued for war, the British, exhausted after nearly two decades of war, were little disposed to follow through.[40] Jackson's political enemies in the United States, some jealous of his military success, felt the same way. Was he acting like another Napoleon? Where would his expansionist policies erupt next?

Congress set about investigating his actions. On January 12, 1819, the House military committee recommended Jackson be censured for his highhanded actions in Florida. Hearing of the congressional attempt to censure him, Jackson made his way to Washington to lobby in his own defense. House Speaker Henry Clay led the anti-Jackson faction. The debate raged for over nearly a month. In the final vote, on February 8, 1819, Jackson prevailed. He was exonerated on the charges of executing Arbuthnot and Ambrister and illegally invading Florida and taking Pensacola.

No one wanted to challenge the hero of New Orleans and the victor of the Seminole War. He would spend nearly the next two years traveling around the country, receiving accolades, and resting his body.[41]

With the conclusion of the military aspects of the campaign, the diplomatic negotiations began. Certainly Spain was in no position to retaliate militarily. It had been engaged in a war of independence with its subjects in Central and South America, and by 1824 Spain would lose nearly all of its former colonies. Future president John Quincy Adams, son of the second president, undertook the delicate negotiation with the Spanish foreign minister, Don Luis de Onis. On February 22, 1819, the Adams-Onis Treaty (also known as the Transcontinental Treaty) was signed in Washington and approved by the Senate on February 24. Spain, however, refused to sign until February 1821 at which time the Senate again ratified the treaty that ceded Florida to the United States.[42]

When Monroe learned that the Spanish monarch had accepted the treaty, he asked Jackson to be the first governor of Florida. Although in poor health, with the bullet in his chest paining him terribly, Jackson was not prone to accept the position. Then Secretary of War Calhoun appealed to his patriotism by writing the situation, "will require a military eye as its defences ought to receive early and prompt attention."[43] The tired, ill general desired to spend more time with Rachael and pursue his interests in farming and horse breeding. Never a wealthy man, he frankly needed to make his plantation prosperous. Yet he realized as governor he would encourage immigration and set to rest all past criticism of his actions there. In February, 1821, he was appointed governor and on June 1, 1821, he formally tendered his resignation as Major General. Even as his military career ended, his political career was just beginning.

Jackson arrived early in June to assume the position of territorial governor of Florida. Immediately upon his arrival he created another international incident. The new governor—ever the defender of damsels in distress—had taken up the cause of a poor woman who claimed she had been swindled out of her inheritance through economic malfeasance by a British company. Because Jose Callava, the last Spanish governor, would not allow Jackson free access to the Spanish archives, he seized Callava in the night and jailed him. Although Callava was released the next day, critics called it another example of boorish behavior. Others more philosophically claimed that "at least he had not hanged anybody—this time." [44] His tenure as governor lasted about twelve weeks. He arrived back in Nashville, to a hero's welcome, on November 7. Monroe officially accepted his letter of resignation on December 1, 1821.

Unofficially the federal government was glad to see Jackson retire. He caused officials no small amount of headaches. The people, however, were of a different mind. The now fifty-four-year-old was their champion, their hero, the most popular man in America, and they would not let him long languish in Nashville. He was much too popular for that. All overt criticism of Jackson, for the moment, vanished. He was again a hero.

Wherever he went throughout the country, immense crowds greeted him and cheered lustily. Songs were written in his honor, and in Baltimore when he appeared, the band struck up "See the conquering hero comes!" The hero of New Orleans was now the hero of Florida. At a banquet in Nashville, no less than twenty-seven toasts were drunk in his honor. "Among the people," opined one newspaper, ". . . his popularity is unbounded—old and young speak of him with rapture." [45]

CHAPTER EIGHTEEN

Jackson as President

"Well, for Mr. Jackson's sake, I am glad; for my part, I never wished it."

—Rachel Jackson on hearing he had become president

THE POLITICAL QUESTION in 1824 was this: Could the hero of New Orleans parlay his personal popularity into the highest office in the land? Was 1824 the year when popularly elected candidates and not those chosen by congressional caucuses could win? With the adoption of the Constitution in 1787, only adult white male property owners participated in the political process (it was not until July 1971 with the passage of the Twenty-sixth Amendment that lowered the voting age to eighteen that the last of these restrictions ended). The belief was that the common citizen could not be trusted with power. In 1824, however, most states were dropping the property requirement, thus expanding the electorate. Also by 1824, the "era of good feelings" was over. The crumbling Republican Party was split by sectionalism and fractious personalities. Jackson and three other candidates—Secretary of State John Quincy Adams from Massachusetts, Speaker of the House Henry Clay of Kentucky, and Secretary of the Treasury William Crawford from Georgia—vied for the popular vote.

Andrew Jackson won both the popular and the electoral votes, but failed to acquire the necessary majority in the Electoral College. The election then went to the House of Representatives where each state had one vote. There Jackson lost. Clay threw his support behind Adams, who then had the necessary majority. Five days after winning the election, Adams appointed Clay secretary of state. Jackson was furious. He believed Clay betrayed the voice of the people, who clearly wanted Jackson. "So you see the *Judas* of the West has closed the contract," complained Old Hickory to a friend, "and will receive the thirty pieces of silver."[1] The two men became bitter enemies. "He is certainly the bases[t], meanest, scoundrel that ever disgraced the image of god," Jackson ranted to Sam Houston nearly two years after the election, "nothing too mean or low for him to condescend to."[2] Jackson's supporters believed a deal had been struck, and the expression "Corrupt Bargain" became the campaign slogan for the next four years. Led by New Yorker Martin Van Buren, Jackson's followers began what would soon become the Democratic Party and began preparations for the election of 1828.

Campaigning for the election of 1828 began immediately

after the election of 1824. The emerging Democratic Party portrayed itself as the party of the people and characterized Adams and his supporters as corrupt and representative of the aristocratic elite who manipulated the system for their own gain. The main political issues of the time involved the competing interests of sectionalism. The urbanizing North relied on small farms, commerce, and a growing industrial base protected by tariffs. It was to their advantage to have a strong centralized government capable of advancing these issues. The mainly rural South and West, on the other hand, supported large slaveholding agricultural interests, westward expansion, and individual and states' rights. These issues became blurred by the personalities involved. This election proved to be one of the most vitriolic and personal campaigns in American history.

All of Jackson's questionable actions of the past were revived—his voting against accepting Washington's resignation in the House; his actions during the Indian wars, including the execution of the militiamen; his hanging of the British subjects; the legality of the invasion of Florida; his personal duels and the Benton shootout—and all were fodder for the opposition press. Undoubtedly the most damaging and hurtful, however, was the issue of his marriage to Rachel. Reports of her bigamy and Jackson's role in stealing another man's wife filled the news.[3]

The Democrats, who believed Adams stole the election of 1824 fired back. Adams was successful as diplomat to czarist Russia because he pimped for the czar and provided sex slaves to him. He became known as the "Pimp of the Coalition" among the Democrats of the West. He was also accused of recklessly spending the people's money. "Jackson and Reform" became the Democrats' slogan for the next four years as the country divided, largely upon sectional lines. All of the slanderous charges were played out in the press, which became extremely partisan.[4] Jackson, however, the military hero and advocate of westward expansion, had won the hearts of the people and they went to the polls in droves to support him.

In November 1828, the people's candidate, Andrew Jackson, was elected the seventh president of the United States. He received 56 percent of the popular vote. The margin in the Electoral College was 178 to 83. Adams won New England, about half of New York's votes, New Jersey, Delaware, and Maryland. All of the South and West went for Jackson and his reform. The Age of Jackson had begun.[5]

When news of the victory reached the Hermitage, all rejoiced except Rachel. "Well, for Mr. Jackson's sake," she quietly whispered, "I am glad; for my part, I never wished it."[6] She would never make it to the White House. For the last five years her health had deteriorated. She complained of pains around her heart and needed frequent rest. A pious and kind woman by nature, she was greatly affected by the poisonous political campaign. Her husband tried to protect her from the raging rumors in the press. When she finally read the terrible accusations concerning her and Andrew's marriage, she sobbed hysterically. On June 1, 1828, their adopted Indian son, Lyncoya, died, which added to her grief. On the morning of December 17, 1828, while talking with her maid, Hannah, she "uttered a horrible shriek, placed her hands upon her heart, sunk into a chair, struggling for breath, and fell forward into Hannah's arms."[7] Quickly she was taken to her bed, and Jackson was sent for. For five days she vacillated between life and death. Her devoted Andrew never left her side. Finally on December 22, the exhausted Jackson went for some rest. Feeling better, Rachel was placed on a chair, supported by Hannah, while they changed the bedding. Suddenly she suffered another attack and uttered a "long, loud, inarticulate cry; which was immediately followed by a rattling noise in her throat."[8] She never regained consciousness. "Bleed her," cried the anguished Jackson. When no blood flowed from her arm, the distraught husband yelled, "Try the temple, Doctor." Only two drops stained her cap. She had died. He spent the entire night by her side.[9] Rachel was interred in the garden of the Hermitage on Christmas Eve. The general was never the same. He mourned her loss until the day he died and never forgave the people whom he believed had been responsible by their words.

Upon taking the oath of office, Jackson believed he had a mandate from the people. He was the representative of the "common man"; he spoke for and defended their interests as no one had done before. The first president born in a log cabin, orphaned before the age of fifteen, and hardened by decades of military campaigning, he was the prototype of the self-made man. He strengthened the office of the president previously dominated by Congress. The legislative branch of government had to contend with a strong leader and one who knew how to use his constitutional powers to the fullest. During his first term, he exercised his veto power over legislation more than all the previous presidents combined. He could not, however, change his nature.

He ran his government like he ran his army. He was in charge, and one was either for him or against him. As in the military with its frequent rotation of officers, he began what has been labeled the *spoils system*. Bureaucrats left too long in a position become dictatorial and complacent. Periodic replacement would keep them sharp and compliant to the wishes of the president. One person whom Jackson wanted to replace was his vice president, John C. Calhoun.

One of Jackson's biggest challenges was the issue of nullification and the growing underlying problem of sectionalism. At its root, government seeks to answer the question: Who's in charge here? At this time the debate was between local and state governments versus the growing authority of the federal government. If a law was passed inimical to the interests of the states, were they required to comply with it? Calhoun was a firm believer in states' rights; he was the chief supporter of the doctrine of nullification. This principle supported a state's right to nullify, or not obey, a federal law that it believed was detrimental. Talk of secession from the Union filled the news. Jackson opposed any talk of dissolving the Union, however, and was prepared to use force if necessary. At a dinner on April 13, 1830, commemorating Thomas Jefferson's birthday, the issue came to a head. When it was time for Jackson to toast, he made his position known. "Our Union—it must be preserved," he toasted while looking at Calhoun. The vice president then arose, looked squarely back at him, and answered, "The Union—next to our liberty most dear."[10]

Astutely the now politician and statesman Jackson resolved the issue and postponed the breakup of the Union for another thirty years. Publicly he threatened to hang anyone who spoke of disunion and prepared to send forces to South Carolina if the state did secede. "Nullification therefore means insurrection and war," the general wrote Joel Poinsett in December 1832, "and the other states have a right to put it down."[11] Privately he worked to reduce the tariff that was the main bone of contention. As 1833 began, both a Force Bill (called the "Bloody Bill" or the "War Bill" by southerners) authorizing the use of force to quell any rebellion and a bill lowering the tariffs were introduced. Slowly but surely cooler heads prevailed. South Carolina received little encouragement from other states and was not about to face the wrath of the United States military alone. Jackson, by his swift political action and military threat, had averted this crisis.[12] Weeks before Jackson died, his pastor, Dr. Edgar, asked him what he would have done had Calhoun and the nullifiers not backed down. "Hung them sir," he immediately responded, "as high as Haman."[13]

Jackson also took on the influential and wealthy Nicholas Biddle, president of the Second National Bank. This bank was chartered by Madison in 1816 and served as the depository for US Treasury funds. In 1832, Jackson vetoed the bank's charter and the next year began depositing all US funds into state and local banks. The death sentence for the national bank came when its charter officially ended in 1836. Jackson's opposition to the bank stemmed from his belief that it favored wealthy northeasterners over the agrarian South and West. Funding for westward expansion was held up or denied. The banks also controlled the money supply, and many politicians were in its pocket. Moreover, it was run for personal profit, not the good of the people.

When the president ordered Secretary of the Treasury William J. Duane to remove US deposits from the bank, Duane refused and declined to resign as ordered. This action raised the issue of whether a president could fire a member of his cabinet who had been confirmed by the Senate. Although this issue appears inconceivable to modern readers (Lincoln and Andrew Johnson also had to fight Congress over this issue), it had not been resolved at this time. The old soldier's hackles again rose. The cabinet worked for him (and by extension the people) and not Congress. He fired Duane and appointed Roger B. Taney, who followed his orders.[14] On April 4, 1834, the House declared the Bank of the United Staes, "ought not to be recharted."[15] (On March 26, the Senate passed a resolution of censure against Jackson for exceeding his authority on this action. Opponents labeled him "King Andrew" and denounced his high-handed ways. When Democrats again controlled Congress in 1837, the censure was expunged.) In effect the bank was now dead and executive power, though still highly contested, had taken another leap forward. Controversy, however, was far from being over for Jackson.

The issue for which Jackson's name is still reviled in many parts of the country, especially among Native Americans, is

Indian removal. By 1830, approximately six thousand members of the so-called five civilized tribes had accepted the government's offer to move across the Mississippi into Oklahoma, far fewer than anticipated or desired. Settlers pressed their demands on the federal government to do something to open up the eastern lands still in Indian possession. Always sympathetic to southern and western demands, President Jackson determined to do something once and for all about the situation. In 1830, under Jackson's urgings, Congress passed the General Removal Act, which in effect ordered the removal of all eastern tribes to the West. It made little difference to Old Hickory that many Native Americans had attempted to assimilate into white culture. The issue now was the acquisition of their remaining land.[16] The fulfillment of this law was a shameful and unjust mess.

Although Sharp Knife became the focal point of indignation, he was carrying out the policy desired by the white majority and espoused as long ago as 1803 by Jefferson. He knew the remaining Indians could not survive in their present situation. Slowly, yet inexorably, especially since the War of 1812 and Jackson's subsequent incursions into the Gulf area, Indian land and the Indian way of life were disappearing Over the next several years the states began a systematic policy of forcing the tribes to negotiate a treaty that stripped them of their lands and forced them to move.

By 1830, many tribes had adopted the white educational system, owned businesses, and became Christianized. They were not, however, subject to state laws and were sovereign in their own territory. Threatened, the state governments, beginning with Mississippi, implemented the provisions of the Removal Act against the Choctaws, and by 1833 about 11,000 were removed. Many perished for lack of food, shelter, and illness when a cholera epidemic broke out. In 1832, the Chickasaws agreed to leave their homes and join the Choctaws, and nearly all 4,900 (with their 1,150 slaves) had arrived in Oklahoma by 1838.[17]

In 1832, the Creeks signed a treaty dissolving the Creek nation in Alabama. Their choice was to either move west with Creeks already there or remain under state law on an allotted parcel of land. The results of those who remained confirmed the fears of Jackson. Not having a concept of private ownership of land, the Indians were soon swindled out of their land and left destitute. In 1836, after a brief rebellion that forced Jackson to send federal troops to Alabama, those involved in the uprising that did not escape to Florida were removed in chains. Estimates run as high as three thousand dead during the trek culminating in 1836 with about fifteen thousand arriving in Oklahoma.[18]

The Seminoles, who resided in Florida, southern Georgia, and Alabama, also signed a treaty in 1832 that stated they would leave for the West. The Florida Seminoles, however, had other ideas. The Second Seminole War, led by Chief Osceola, lasted from late 1835 to 1842. By the end of this war, nearly four thousand Seminoles had been removed.[19]

The Cherokees chose a different means to fight removal. As early as 1831, the Cherokees had attempted to legally block removal. In the court case *Cherokee Nation v. Georgia*, on March 18, 1831, Chief Justice John Marshall ruled the Indians were not subject to state laws, but Indian lands were part of the United

States. They were defined as "domestic dependent nations." The military should be used to protect Indian rights, not evict them. Jackson is reputed to have defiantly said of this verdict, "Well: John Marshall has made his decision: *now let him enforce it!*"[20] It may be legend—but it sounds like Jackson.

The beginning of the end of this tragedy occurred in late December 1835 when the Cherokee nation signed the treaty to move west. During this year, nearly two thousand Cherokees, members of what was called the Treaty Party, peacefully relocated to Oklahoma. Followers of another Cherokee faction, led by John Ross, however, refused to budge. By the fall of 1838, President Martin Van Buren ordered the nation rounded up and sent west along what is known as the Trail of Tears. Cold weather, inadequate provisions, and hostile whites along the way took their toll. Estimates are that some four thousand of the eighteen thousand Cherokees, mainly the very old or very young, died as a result of this removal. More died the following year because little preparation had been made for their arrival in a hostile environment.[21] Although Van Buren actually carried out the most shameful part of the removal, Jackson initiated the policy.

In all it is estimated that by the end of his two terms as president, Jackson's policy had removed 45,690 Indians across the Mississippi.[22] The number of deaths occurring as a result of removal is unknown. Certainly the degree of human misery, suffering, and loss of loved ones as well as property is impossible to calculate. Strong feelings of hatred for Jackson exist among many Native Americans to this day, and his policy of Indian removal is one of his most controversial legacies. There is no question it remains a shameful blot on the history of this nation.

It is difficult for us today to understand how this policy could have been carried out. Jackson honestly believed he did the right thing by sending the Indians west. He fulfilled the desires of the white majority, acquired about one hundred million acres of land for the United States, ended all possible Indian alliances with foreign governments in the South, and brought peace to an often war-torn, violent area. He also affirmed the rights of states to have authority over all inhabitants within their borders. In addition, he allowed for the possibility of the continuance of the Native American culture and way of life by placing them in a location unaffected by white civilization. In 1834, he oversaw the legislation that established the Office of Indian Affairs. Headed by an Indian, this agency reformed and standardized policies and brought order to an otherwise incoherent system.

The significance of Jackson's presidency cannot be overstated. For the first time the common man had a champion in the White House. The caucus system whereby congressional committees chose the candidate with no regard for popular opinion was ended. The precedent of a poor rural man, with little formal education, arising from the ranks of the military to become president was established. Although he was labeled "King Andrew" by his political rivals because of his sometimes autocratic approach, the executive branch of government, long dominated by the legislative branch, came into its own. The use of the presidential veto, used more often by Jackson than all previous presidents combined, became a political tool. The banking system, long dominated by a wealthy few, was ended. The Democratic Party, one that listened to the demands of the landless workers, emerged; to counteract it, the Whigs sprang on the scene in 1834. Perhaps most significantly, the Age of Jackson fanned the debate, continuing to the present, over the role and power of the federal government versus those of state and local governments as well as the role of the executive versus the legislative branch of government.

Courtesy of the Library of Congress

The British fleet bombarding Fort McHenry, September 13–14, 1814. Francis Scott Key, an American lawyer negotiating an exchange of prisoners onboard a British ship, observed the battle and penned the "Star-Spangled Banner."

Aseola, Chief of the
Seminole nation.

Andrew Jackson
as President of the
United States.

CHAPTER NINETEEN

Legacy

"Heaven will be no heaven to me if I do not meet my wife there."

—Jackson speaking about his beloved Rachel

Andrew Jackson quietly died on Sunday, June 1, 1845. Two weeks before that day, the bedridden invalid took Communion with his family. "Death has no terror for me," he quietly told them. "When I have suffered sufficiently, the Lord will take me to himself; but what are my sufferings compared with those of the blessed Saviour who died on the accursed tree for me? Mine are nothing."[1] Jackson viewed his life as a struggle, and suffering played a large role in shaping his nature, faith, and military career. He never ran from confrontation or controversy. From his youth the general had to swim upstream and overcome obstacles to succeed. He died as perhaps the most popular man in America, certainly on par with Washington and Jefferson. In 1855, Congress ordered the first public statue of a citizen erected in the nation's capital—Jackson astride his horse. Washington's statue came years later. Present-day historians may dispute his actions as being high-handed, racist, or egomaniacal, but his devotion to duty as he saw it, strengthened by an indomitable will, guided him.

President James A. Garfield once said, "A pound of pluck is worth a ton of luck." Andrew Jackson would have agreed. Through sheer force of will, raw ambition, a clear sense of his purpose, coupled with his faith in the American people and the support of his Rachel and the belief in his God, combined with "a ton of luck," he thrived and became a symbol for early nineteenth-century America. Through his aggressive, bold actions, he not only provided the impetus for the domestic spirit of nationalism, but also convincingly put down an initial challenge to the unity of the nation. He elevated the status and pride of the common man, even as he spoke for him. Internationally Jackson affirmed America's ability to defend itself against the most formidable power in the world and raised respect for its principles and people. Where did the pluck come from? Wherein lies his greatness? What lessons does his life provide for us today?

Although many of his words and actions may have belied it, Jackson was a man of faith. Throughout his life, he attended church, gave alms, read the Scripture, and supported preachers. At Rachel's request he built a chapel at the Hermitage. As he approached the end of his life, his faith became more apparent and public. When at home on the Sabbath, he would say to his frequent guests, "Gentlemen, do what you please in my house; *I* am going to church."[2] He promised Rachel that once he was out of politics, for he did not want his enemies to use his faith as a political weapon, he would make a public profession of faith and join the Presbyterian Church.[3] He did that in 1839 after resolving one great stumbling block—forgiveness. After discussing doctrine and his beliefs, Dr. John Edgar, his friend and pastor, asked Jackson if he could forgive his enemies. "My political enemies I can freely forgive," he responded. But those who attacked him "*for* serving my country—Doctor, that is a different case," he protested.[4] After further discussion, Jackson confessed he could forgive *all* his enemies. The next Sunday, leaning heavily upon his stick and his eyes filled with tears, Jackson answered the required questions, promised to fulfill the requirements of the church, and was pronounced a member. For the rest of his life, he spent time daily reading the Bible, praying, and attending services.

He was also a man in love. Next to his duty to his country, which always took precedence, his love for Rachel was most important in his life. His devotion to Rachel, although he spent much time away from her, is a great love story. His letters were full of words of love and devotion. Even after her death, he revered her memory. While walking in Jackson's garden and discussing his will with him, a friend asked if Jackson thought it proper to leave everything to his son, Andrew Jr. After reflecting a moment, he pointed at Rachel's tomb and replied, "If *she* were alive, she would wish him to have it all, and to me her wish is law."[5] On another occasion while talking about Rachel, he remarked, "Heaven will be no heaven to me if I do not meet my wife there."[6] As he approached the end of his days, he ordered his body to be laid beside that of Rachel at the Hermitage.

Jackson has frequently been called a "man of the people." Yet this egalitarianism did not conflict with his military views. He was in charge, but he shared every hardship with his men. No other general in history suffered physically as much as he did in the field. Since 1813, his body contained two bullets; he suffered constantly from diarrhea and dyspepsia. Nevertheless, he gave up his horse to walk while the wounded rode.[7] No general required more of his men. He executed some and threatened to shoot others, but they loved him and fought and died for him. He reveled in his successes—yet always praised and credited his soldiers with the victories. He did not interfere with his officers as long as they carried out his orders and performed their duty. His military greatness lies not so much in his being a brilliant tactician, but in being a natural-born leader able to make decisions, usually successful, on the spot and to do his duty as he saw it. The intangible "luck," which he thanked on many occasions, was also on his side.

Just before he died, with the room full of family, servants, and friends, Jackson put on his glasses and looked around. "God will take care of you for me," he quietly spoke. "I am my God's. I belong to him, I go but a short time before you, and I want to meet you all in heaven, both black and white."[8] All burst into tears. A few hours later he died. According to Remini, these words impressed the hearers, and they were printed in newspapers and contained in several letters.[9] Sam Houston arrived with his wife and son at the Hermitage the day Jackson died. After they kneeled at his bed and looked at his face, Houston said, "My son, try to remember that you have looked on the face of Andrew Jackson."[10]

In a eulogy of Andrew Jackson delivered in New York, perhaps Benjamin F. Butler best summarized his life: "I feel it right to state my entire conviction that . . . in every act of his public life, he proceeded under a deep sense of what he believed to be the injunction of duty; and duty was ever to him as the voice of heaven."[11]

His simple tombstone reads: General Andrew Jackson, Born March 15, 1767–Died June 8, 1845.

Notes

PROLOGUE

    1. Robert Remini, *The Life of Andrew Jackson* (New York: Harper & Row, 1988), 178.

    2. Margaret Bayard Smith (Mrs. Samuel Harrison Smith), *The First Forty Years of Washington Society*, ed. Gaillard Hunt (New York: Charles Scribner's Sons, 1906), 292.

    3. James Parton, *Life of Andrew Jackson*, vol. 3 (New York: Mason Brothers, 1860), 169. Parton is considered one of America's first serious biographers.

    4. Ibid.

    5. Smith, *The First Forty Years*, 290–91.

    6. Ibid., 293.

    7. Ibid., 294.

    8. Parton, *Life of Andrew Jackson*, 3:170.

    9. Ronald E. Shaw, ed., *Andrew Jackson, 1767–1845, Chronology, Documents, Bibliographical Aids* (Dobbs Ferry, NY: Oceana Publications, 1969), 21–22.

    10. Parton, *Life of Andrew Jackson*, 3:291.

    11. Smith, *The First Forty Years*, 294.

    12. Parton, *Life of Andrew Jackson*, 3:169.

    13. Smith, *The First Forty Years*, 295.

    14. Quoted in Jon Meacham, *American Lion: Andrew Jackson in the White*

House (New York: Random House, 2008), 62.

15. Parton, *Life of Andrew Jackson*, 3:170–71.

16. Smith, *The First Forty Years*, 296.

17. Marquis James, *The Life of Andrew Jackson* according to Bibliography, Complete in One Volume (New York: Bobbs-Merrill, 1938), 187.

18. Parton, *Life of Andrew Jackson*, 3:170–71.

19. James, *Life of Andrew Jackson*, 187.

20. Parton, *Life of Andrew Jackson*, 3:170–71.

21. Arthur Schlesinger Jr., *The Age of Jackson*; and John W. Ward, *Andrew Jackson: Symbol for an Age*, are two books making this point. Concerning those "who hate him," the author lives now in Oklahoma, the home of the Cherokees forced to relocate in what is called the "Trail of Tears." I have interviewed several descendants of those refugees who to this day refuse to carry a twenty-dollar bill because Jackson's picture is on it.

CHAPTER 1: A BOY BECOMES A MAN

1. Quoted in Augustus C. Buell, *History of Andrew Jackson: Pioneer, Patriot, Soldier, Politician, President* (New York: Charles Scribner's Sons, 1904), 25.

2. James Parton, *Life of Andrew Jackson*, vol. 1 (New York: Mason Brothers, 1860), 47–48.

3. Ibid., 1:49.

4. Hendrik Booraem, *Young Hickory: The Making of Andrew Jackson* (Dallas: Taylor Trade Publishing, 2001), 9, states the elder Jackson "acquired property on the northern fringe of the Waxhaw," amounting to 200 acres.

5. Marquis James, *The Life of Andrew Jackson* according to Bibliography, Complete in one volume (New York: Bobbs-Merrill, 1938), 10.

6. Parton, *Life of Andrew Jackson*, 1:52.

7. Robert Remini, *The Life of Andrew Jackson* (New York: Harper & Row, 1988), 5.

8. Parton, *Life of Andrew Jackson*, 1:58.

9. For a lengthy discussion of the birthplace issue, see James, *Life of Andrew Jackson*, 506–12, and Booraem, *Young Hickory*, 10–14.

10. Jon Meacham, *American Lion: Andrew Jackson in the White House* (New York: Random House, 2008), 17.

11. Ibid., 9, 18. The Westminster Shorter Catecheism is formatted in a series of more than one hundred short questions and answers. For example, number one is: Q: "What is the chief end of man?" A: "Man's chief end is to glorify God and enjoy him forever." Number seventeen is Q: "Into what estate

did the fall bring mankind?" A: "The fall brought mankind into the estate of sin and misery." http://www.reformed.org/documents/WSC frames.html, accessed online January 17, 2011.

12. Buell, *History of Andrew Jackson*, 35.

13. Parton, *Life of Andrew Jackson*, 1:60–61.

14. Ibid., 1:61.

15. Remini, *Life of Andrew Jackson*, 7.

16. John Reid and John Henry Eaton, *The Life of Andrew Jackson*, ed. Frank Lawrence Owsley Jr. (Tuscaloosa: University of Alabama Press, 1974), 10.

17. Parton, *Life of Andrew Jackson*, 1:67.

18. Quoted in Meacham, *American Lion*, 18.

19. Parton, *Life of Andrew Jackson*, 1:64.

20. Ibid.

21. Ibid., 1:59–60.

22. Ibid., 1:64.

23. Ibid.

24. James Parton, *Life of Andrew Jackson*, vol. 3 (New York: Mason Brothers, 1860), 159.

25. Buell, *History of Andrew Jackson*, 38. Booraem, *Young Hickory*, 201–4, painstakingly details Buell's flawed scholarship.

26. Remini, *Life of Andrew Jackson*, 8.

27. George Scheer and Hugh Rankin, *Rebels and Redcoats* (Cleveland: World Publishing, 1957), 402.

28. Quoted in James, *Life of Andrew Jackson*, 22.

29. Parton, *Life of Andrew Jackson*, 1:88.

30. Ibid., 1:89. Parton states these may not have been the actual words but convey the sentiment.

31. Ibid.

32. Andrew Jackson, *The Papers of Andrew Jackson*, ed. Sam B. Smith and Harriet Chappell Owsley, vol. 1 (Knoxville: University of Tennessee Press, 1980), 7.

33. Quoted in James, *Life of Andrew Jackson*, 30.

34. Parton, *Life of Andrew Jackson*, 1:95.

35. Quoted in James, *Life of Andrew Jackson*, 31.

CHAPTER 2: A LAWYER IS BORN

1. Andrew Jackson, *The Papers of Andrew Jackson*, ed. Sam B. Smith and Harriet Chappell Owsley, vol. 1 (Knoxville: University of Tennessee Press, 1980), 7.

2. Ibid. Jackson remarked later that he thought he "would have made a pretty good saddler."

3. James Parton, *Life of Andrew Jackson*, vol. 1 (New York: Mason Brothers, 1860), 97.

4. Quoted in Jon Meacham, *American Lion: Andrew Jackson in the White House* (New York: Random House, 2008), 15.

5. Robert Remini, *The Life of Andrew Jackson* (New York: Harper & Row, 1988), 10.

6. Parton, *Life of Andrew Jackson*, 1:104–5.

7. Remini, *Life of Andrew Jackson*, 10–11.

8. Parton, *Life of Andrew Jackson*, 1:108.

9. Quoted in ibid., 1:109.

10. Jackson, *Papers*, 1:10.

11. Parton, *Life of Andrew Jackson*, 1:119. Remini (*Life of Andrew Jackson*, 12) states it was Bennett Searcy, Tom's brother.

12. S. G. Heiskill, *Andrew Jackson and Early Tennessee History* (Nashville: Ambrose Printing, 1912), 432.

13. Jackson, *Papers*, 1:15. This page contains the copy of the bill of sale. N. 1 indicates that from 1788 to 1803, he obtained nineteen slaves and sold four; he also "hired" two at the end of 1803 for a year's work.

14. Ibid., 1:12. When possible, I shall use the language and spelling of Jackson to give the flavor of his language as I have done here.

15. Parton, *Life of Andrew Jackson*, 1:162.

16. Ibid., 1:163. About midnight a fire broke out in the town. Jackson organized the fire brigade that saved the town from complete destruction.

17. Parton, *Life of Andrew Jackson*, 1:122–23.

CHAPTER 3: RACHEL AND NASHVILLE

1. A. W. Putnam, *History of Middle Tennessee* or, Life and Times of Gen. James Robertson (Nashville: A. W. Putnam, 1859), 68.

2. Ibid., 74.

3. Ibid., 73.

4. James Parton, *Life of Andrew Jackson*, vol. 1 (New York: Mason Brothers, 1860), 133.

5. S. G. Heiskill, *Andrew Jackson and Early Tennessee History* (Nashville: Ambrose Printing, 1920), 442.

6. Parton, *Life of Andrew Jackson*.

7. Heiskill, *Andrew Jackson and Early Tennessee History*, 442.

8. Andrew Jackson, *The Papers of Andrew Jackson*, ed. Harold D. Moser,

Sharon Macpherson, and Charles F. Bryan Jr., vol. 2 (Knoxville: University of Tennessee Press, 1894), 13.

9. Parton, *Life of Andrew Jackson*, 1:168.

10. Ibid., 1:169.

11. Quoted in Heiskill, *Andrew Jackson and Early Tennessee History*, 446; and Parton, *Life of Andrew Jackson*, 1:150.

12. See Jon Meacham, *American Lion: Andrew Jackson in the White House* (New York: Random House, 2008), 22–24, 383n22; Robert Remini, *The Life of Andrew Jackson* (New York: Harper & Row, 1988), 22–27.

13. Quoted in Remini, *Life of Andrew Jackson*, 24.

14. Parton, *Life of Andrew Jackson*, 1:135.

15. Ibid., 1:139.

16. A. W. Putnam, *History of Middle Tennessee or, Life and Times of Gen. James Robertson* (Knoxville: University of Tennessee Press, 1971), reprint 317–18.

17. Ibid., 318.

18. In February 1789, Jackson wrote a letter to Daniel Smith, commander of the militia. In it he declared peace with the Indians was the "only immediate way" to allow for safe trade. Andrew Jackson, *The Papers of Andrew Jackson*, vol. 1, ed. Sam B. Smith and Harriet Chappell Owsley (Knoxville: University of Tennessee Press, 1980), 6. Five years later, due to the constant fighting, his attitude changed. In a letter to John McKee, he wrote, "Peace Talks are only Delusions." Jackson, *Papers*, 1:48–49.

19. Jackson, *Papers*, 1:26.

20. Parton, *Life of Andrew Jackson*, 1:157.

21. Ibid., 1:155.

22. J. G. M. Ramsey, *The Annals of Tennessee to the End of the Eighteenth Century* (Philadelphia: Walker & James, 1853), 648.

23. Jackson, *Papers*, 1:85.

24. Parton, *Life of Andrew Jackson*, 1:197.

25. Jackson, *Papers*, 1:74.

CHAPTER 4: THE DUELING JUDGE

1. James Parton, *Life of Andrew Jackson*, vol. 1 (New York: Mason Brothers, 1860), 196.

2. William Blount, *Biographical Directory of the United States Congress*, http://bioguide.gov/scripts/biodisplay.pl?index=b000570, accessed February 4, 2011.

3. Andrew Jackson, *The Papers of Andrew Jackson*, vol. 1, ed. Sam B.

Smith and Harriet Chappell Owsley (Knoxville: University of Tennessee Press, 1980), 152.

4. Ibid., 1:91–92.

5. Marquis James, *The Life of Andrew Jackson,* Complete in One Volume (New York: Bobbs-Merrill, 1938), 91. Robert Remini states that Jackson at one time had 150 slaves at the Hermitage. *The Life of Andrew Jackson* (New York: Harper & Row, 1988), 51.

6. Parton, *Life of Andrew Jackson*, 1:219.

7. Ibid., 1:227.

8. See Parton, *Life of Andrew Jackson*, for the legend (228–29) and the actual facts about Bean (166–67). James, *Life of Andrew Jackson*, gives a slightly different version (92).

9. Jackson, *Papers*, 1:290.

10. Parton, *Life of Andrew Jackson*, 1:164.

11. Jackson, *Papers*, 1:367.

12. Ibid., 1:369.

13. Ibid., 1:378–79.

14. Parton, *Life of Andrew Jackson*, 1:234–35; the series of letters is found in Jackson, *Papers*, 1:367–84.

15. Robert Remini, *Andrew Jackson and the Course of American Empire, 1767–1821* (New York: Harper & Row, 1977), 159.

16. Andrew Jackson, *The Papers of Andrew Jackson*, vol. 2, ed. Harold D. Moser, Sharon Macpherson, and Charles F. Bryan Jr. (Knoxville: University of Tennessee Press, 1984), 77–78; the letters between the two are in ibid., 2:79–103.

17. Ibid., 2:100.

18. James, *Life of Andrew Jackson*, 124–25.

19. Amos Kendall, *The Life of Andrew Jackson* (New York: Harper & Brothers, 1843).

20. James, *Life of Andrew Jackson*, 125; Parton, *Life of Andrew Jackson*, 1:295–301.

CHAPTER 5: HOSTILITY WITH THE CREEKS

1. Andrew Jackson, *The Papers of Andrew Jackson*, vol. 2, ed. Harold D. Moser, Sharon Macpherson, and Charles F. Bryan Jr. (Knoxville: University of Tennessee Press, 1984), 110–11.

2. Ibid., 2:111.

3. Ibid., 2:116.

4. Ibid., 2: 174–76.

5. Ibid., 2:266–67.

6. Ibid., 2:300–301.

7. Ibid., 2:307.

8. Ibid., 2:307–8.

9. Quoted in Robert Remini, *Andrew Jackson: A Biography* (New York: Palgrave Macmillan, 2008), 32.

10. See p. 50.

CHAPTER 6: OLD HICKORY

1. The Federalist Party, begun by the supporters of Alexander Hamilton, had lost the election of 1800 when Jefferson prevented John Adams from reelection. The party suffered national disgrace and never recovered from the Hartford Convention in 1814, where the secession of New England from the United States was discussed.

2. Andrew Jackson, *The Papers of Andrew Jackson*, vol. 2, ed. Harold D. Moser, Sharon Macpherson, and Charles F. Bryan Jr. (Knoxville: University of Tennessee Press, 1984), 320–21.

3. Ibid., 2:339.

4. Ibid., 2:342.

5. James Parton, *Life of Andrew Jackson*, vol. 1 (New York: Mason Brothers, 1860), 368.

6. Ibid., 1:372.

7. Jackson, *Papers*, 2:364. The Jacksons had no natural children. Andrew Jackson Jr. was adopted on December 7, 1809, when three days old. The boy, who had a twin brother, was the nephew of Rachel, being born to Severn and Elizabeth Donelson. She was too weak to nurse both infants and therefore gave the baby to the Jacksons.

8. Quoted from Remini, *Andrew Jackson and American Empire*, 175.

9. Ibid., 2:383–85.

10. Ibid., 2:385–87.

11. Ibid., 2:387.

12. Ibid.

13. Ibid., 2:393.

14. Parton, *Life of Andrew Jackson*, 1:382.

15. Ibid.

16. Ibid., 1:387.

17. Ibid., 1:388.

18. Ibid., 1:388–89.

19. Jackson, *Papers*, 2:413.

20. Parton, *Life of Andrew Jackson*, 1:390.

21. Ibid., 392–93.

22. Jackson, *Papers*, 2:426.

23. Parton, *Life of Andrew Jackson*, 1:394.

24. Parton, *Life of Andrew Jackson*, 1:396.

CHAPTER 7: THE CREEK WAR BEGINS

1. J. F. H. Claiborne, *Mississippi as a Province, Territory and State*, vol. 1 (Jackson, MS: Power & Barksdale, 1880), 317.

2. Ibid..

3. Frank L. Owsley Jr., *Struggle for the Gulf Borderlands: The Creek War and the Battle of New Orleans, 1812–1815* (Tuscaloosa: University of Alabama Press, 2000), 32–33.

4. James Parton, *Life of Andrew Jackson*, vol. 1 (New York: Mason Brothers, 1860), 411–12.

5. Quoted in H. W. Brands, *Andrew Jackson: His Life and Times* (New York: Doubleday, 2005), 194.

6. Albert J. Pickett, *The History of Alabama*, vol. 2 (Charleston: Walker & James, 1851), 275.

7. Quoted in Parton, *Life of Andrew Jackson*, 1:420.

8. John Reid and John Henry Eaton, *The Life of Andrew Jackson* (Philadelphia: Carey & Son, 1817).

9. Andrew Jackson, *The Papers of Andrew Jackson*, vol. 2, ed. Harold D. Moser, Sharon Macpherson, and Charles F. Bryan Jr. (Knoxville: University of Tennessee Press, 1984), 428.

10. Ibid., 2:429.

11. Reid and Eaton, *Life of Andrew Jackson*, 33–34.

12. Owsley, *Struggle for the Gulf Borderlands*, 43–45.

13. Jackson, *Papers*, 2:437.

14. Quoted in Robert Remini, *Andrew Jackson and the Course of American Empire, 1767–1821* (New York: Harper & Row, 1977), 192.

15. Jackson, *Papers*, 2:441.

16. Ibid., 2:439.

17. Ibid., 2:440–41.

18. Quoted in Remini, *Andrew Jackson and American Empire*, 193.

19. Marquis James, *The Life of Andrew Jackson,* Complete in One Volume (New York: Bobbs-Merrill, 1938), 167.

20. Parton, *Life of Andrew Jackson*, 1:436–37.

21. Davy Crockett, *Narrative of the Life of Davy Crockett* (Baltimore: Carey & Hart, 1834), 74.

22. Ibid., 88.
23. Ibid., 89–90.
24. Quoted in Parton, *Life of Andrew Jackson*, 1:438.
25. Quoted in ibid., 1:439.
26. Jackson, *Papers*, 2:516.
27. Robert Remini, *The Life of Andrew Jackson* (New York: Harper & Row, 1988), 169.

CHAPTER 8: OLD HICKORY FACES MUTINY

1. James Parton, *Life of Andrew Jackson*, vol. 1 (New York: Mason Brothers, 1860), 441.
2. John Reid and John Henry Eaton, *The Life of Andrew Jackson* (Philadelphia: Carey & Son, 1817), 56.
3. Parton, *Life of Andrew Jackson*, 1:444.
4. Reid and Eaton, *Life of Andrew Jackson*, 60–61.
5. Quoted in Parton, *Life of Andrew Jackson*, 1:446.
6. Quoted in ibid., 1:458.
7. Quoted in Reid and Eaton, *Life of Andrew Jackson*, 66.
8. Ibid., 68.
9. Parton, *Life of Andrew Jackson*, 1:464.
10. Reid and Eaton, *Life of Andrew Jackson*, 69–70; Robert Remini, *Andrew Jackson and the Course of American Empire, 1767–1821* (New York: Harper & Row, 1977), 198–99.
11. Reid and Eaton, *Life of Andrew Jackson*, 78.
12. Ibid., 83.
13. Quoted in Parton, *Life of Andrew Jackson*, 1:471.
14. Quoted in Remini, *Andrew Jackson and American Empire*, 49.
15. Reid and Eaton, *Life of Andrew Jackson*, 102.
16. Ibid., 105–6.
17. Quoted in Remini, *Andrew Jackson and American Empire*, 205.

CHAPTER 9: THE BATTLE OF HORSESHOE BEND

1. Quoted in James Parton, *Life of Andrew Jackson*, vol. 1 (New York: Mason Brothers, 1860), 488.
2. John Reid and John Henry Eaton, *The Life of Andrew Jackson* (Philadelphia: Carey & Son, 1817), 126.
3. Quoted in Parton, *Life of Andrew Jackson*, 1:489.
4. Reid and Eaton, *Life of Andrew Jackson*, 128.
5. Ibid., 129.
6. Ibid., 130.

7. Quoted in Robert Remini, *Andrew Jackson and the Course of American Empire, 1767–1821* (New York: Harper & Row, 1977), 208.

8. Reid and Eaton, *Life of Andrew Jackson*, 134.

9. Ibid., 136. This account was written by Jackson's friend Major John Eaton. Jackson's aide and friend John Reid died suddenly on January 15, 1816, after completing only four chapters. Eaton finished the book. It was published in 1817 with the proceeds going to Reid's family.

10. Parton, *Life of Andrew Jackson*, 1:498.

11. Remini, *Andrew Jackson and American Empire*, 209–10.

12. Quoted in Parton, *Life of Andrew Jackson*, 1:508.

13. Reid and Eaton, *Life of Andrew Jackson*, 143. Caliber is the measure of the bore of the musket barrel. Thus a .70 caliber had a barrel nearly ? th of an inch and the ball weighed about an ounce. This put a large hole in a man.

14. Ibid., 149.

15. Ibid., 150

16. After the battle Jackson stood over Montgomery's body, wept, and said, "I have lost the flower of my army." Albert J. Pickett, *History of Alabama*, 2 vols. (Charleston: Walker & James, 1851), 2:345.

17. Henry Halbert and T. H. Ball, *The Creek War of 1813 and 1814* (Tuscaloosa: University of Alabama Press, 1995), 276.

18. Pickett, *History of Alabama*, 343–44.

19. Ibid., 342–43.

20. Halbert and Ball, *Creek War*, 277.

21. Ibid., 276–77.

22. Remini, *Andrew Jackson and American Empire*, 216.

CHAPTER 10: THE CREEK WAR ENDS: THE TREATY OF FORT JACKSON

1. John Reid and John Henry Eaton, *The Life of Andrew Jackson* (Philadelphia: Carey & Son, 1817), 157–58.

2. Ibid.

3. Ibid., 165.

4. James Parton, *Life of Andrew Jackson*, vol. 1 (New York: Mason Brothers, 1860), 532.

5. Quoted in ibid., 1:532–33. The same basic story is recounted in Frank L. Owsley Jr., *Struggle for the Gulf Borderlands* (Tuscaloosa: University of Alabama Press, 2000), 84, and Reid and Eaton, *Life of Andrew Jackson*, 165.

6. Parton, *Life of Andrew Jackson*, 1:533.

7. Ibid., 1:534.

8. Reid and Eaton, *Life of Andrew Jackson*, 166.

9. Weatherford's pleas were heard, and five thousand Indians moved north of Fort William. During the summer of 1814, they drew rations from the government, which saved many from starvation. Following the Creek War, Weatherford became a planter and died in 1826 after becoming fatigued following a "desperate bear hunt." Parton, *Life of Andrew Jackson*, 1:535.

10. Reid and Eaton, *Life of Andrew Jackson*, 173–74.

11. Parton, *Life of Andrew Jackson*, 1:542–43.

12. John Spencer Bassett, ed., *The Correspondence of Andrew Jackson*, vol. 2 (Washington, DC: Carnegie Institution of Washington, 1927), 4.

13. Ibid., 2:5.

14. Ibid., 2:9. With the promotion came pay at $2,500 per annum. In addition, he received allowances for servants, feed for his horses, and transportation that bumped the total to more than $6,000.

15. Ibid., 2:9–11.

16. Ibid., 2:12–13.

17. Ibid., 2:13; Armstrong admits that President Madison held up sending the letter but fails to explain why. Perhaps he did so to maintain Spanish neutrality. See Robert Remini, *Andrew Jackson and the Course of American Empire, 1767–1821* (New York: Harper & Row, 1977), 453n57; and Reid and Eaton, *Life of Andrew Jackson*, 197.

18. Quoted in Owsley, *Struggle for the Gulf Borderlands*, 86–87.

19. Reid and Eaton, *Life of Andrew Jackson*, 190–91; Parton, *Life of Andrew Jackson*, 1:553–54.

20. Quoted in Marquis James, *The Life of Andrew Jackson* Complete in One Volume (New York: Bobbs-Merrill, 1938), 190.

CHAPTER 11: FORT BOWYER AND PENSACOLA

1. Quoted in Benson J. Lossing, *The Pictorial Field-Book of the War of 1812*, vol. 2 (New York, 1868), 935–36.

2. Paul Jennings, *A Colored Man's Reminiscences of James Madison* (Brooklyn: George C. Beadle, 1865), 14. http://docsouth.unc.edu/neh/jennings/jennings.html accessed on April 4, 2011.

3. Frank L. Owsley Jr., *Struggle for the Gulf Borderlands* (Tuscaloosa: University of Alabama Press, 2000). Chapter 9 provides excellent details of overall British strategy.

4. John Spencer Bassett, ed., *The Correspondence of Andrew Jackson*, 2 vols. (Washington, DC: Carnegie Institution of Washington, 1927), 2:15–16.

5. Ibid., 2:20–21.

6. Ibid., 2:33–34.

7. Ibid., 2:40.

8. Owsley, *Struggle for the Gulf Borderlands*, 107–9.

9. James Parton, *Life of Andrew Jackson*, vol. 1 (New York: Mason Brothers, 1860), 606–8; John Reid and John Henry Eaton, *The Life of Andrew Jackson* (Philadelphia: Carey & Son, 1817), 214–16.

10. Parton, *Life of Andrew Jackson*, 1:610.

11. Bassett, *Correspondence of Andrew Jackson*, 2:50.

12. Ibid., 2:71.

13. Andrew Jackson, *The Papers of Andrew Jackson*, vol. 3, ed. Harold D. Moser, David R. Hoth, Sharon Macpherson, and John H. Reinbold (Knoxville: University of Tennessee Press, 1991), 155.

14. Ibid., 3:169.

15. Ibid., 3:171.

16. Bassett, *Correspondence of Andrew Jackson*, 2:82–83.

17. See Robert Remini, *Andrew Jackson and the Course of American Empire, 1767–1821* (New York: Harper & Row, 1977), 455n21.

18. Bassett, *Correspondence of Andrew Jackson*, 2:92.

19. Ibid., 2:93.

20. Parton, *Life of Andrew Jackson*, 1:620.

21. Jackson, *Papers*, 3:185.

22. Bassett, *Correspondence of Andrew Jackson*, 2:99.

23. Parton, *Life of Andrew Jackson*, 1:623; Bassett, *Correspondence of Andrew Jackson*, 2:104.

24. Ibid., 2:99.

25. Reid and Eaton, *Life of Andrew Jackson*, 235.

CHAPTER 12: NEW ORLEANS: PREPARATION FOR BATTLE

1. Quoted in H. W. Brands, *Andrew Jackson: His Life and Times* (New York: Doubleday, 2005), 249–50.

2. Quoted in Charles Gayarré, *History of Louisiana*, vol. 4 (New York: Redfield & William J. Widdleton, 1854), 380.

3. John Spencer Bassett, ed., *The Correspondence of Andrew Jackson*, 2 vols. (Washington, DC: Carnegie Institution of Washington, 1927), 2:107.

4. Louise Livingston Hunt, *Memoir of Mrs. Edward Livingston with Letters Hitherto Unpublished* (New York: Harper & Brothers, 1886), 52.

5. Alexander Walker, *Jackson and New Orleans: An Authentic Narrative* (New York: J. C. Derby, 1856), 13.

6. Gayarré, *History of Louisiana*, 4:381.

7. Hunt, *Memoir of Mrs. Edward Livingston*, 53.

8. Ibid.

9. Samuel Carter III, *Blaze of Glory* (New York: St. Martin's Press, 1971), 87.

10. Ibid., 91—92.

11. Bassett, *Correspondence of Andrew Jackson*, 2:110.

12. Ibid., 2:58.

13. Benjamin J. Lossing, *The Pictorial Field-Book of the War of 1812*, vol. 2 (New York, 1868), 1018.

14. Major A. Lacarrière Latour, *Historical Memoir of the War in West Florida and Louisiana* (Philadelphia: John Conrad, 1816) appendix, ix—xii.

15. Ibid., 71—72.

16. James Parton, *Life of Andrew Jackson*, vol. 2 (New York: Mason Brothers, 1860), 43.

17. Frank L. Owsley Jr., *Struggle for the Gulf Borderlands* (Tuscaloosa: University of Alabama Press, 2000), 138–39.

18. Ibid., 139; Parton, *Life of Andrew Jackson*, 2:53.

19. Ibid., 2: 60–61.

20. Quoted in Parton, *Life of Andrew Jackson*, 2:70–71.

21. Walker, *Jackson and New Orleans*, 149–50.

22. Ibid., 151.

23. Vincent Nolte, *Fifty Years in Both Hemispheres* (New York: Redfield, 1854), 209–10.

CHAPTER 13: THE BATTLE OF NEW ORLEANS: BEGINNINGS

1. Major A. Lacarrière Latour, *Historical Memoir of the War in West Florida and Louisiana* (Philadelphia: John Conrad, 1816), 112.

2. John Reid and John Henry Eaton, *The Life of Andrew Jackson* (Philadelphia: Carey & Son, 1817), 288.

3. John Spencer Bassett, ed., *The Correspondence of Andrew Jackson*, 2 vols. (Washington, DC: Carnegie Institution of Washington, 1927), 2:126–27; Jane Lucas de Grummond, *The Baratarians and the Battle of New Orleans* (Baton Rouge: LSU Press, 1961), 86–87; Reid and Eaton, *Life of Andrew Jackson*, 290. Daquin's unit was composed of free men of color, most from the island of what is today the Dominican Republic.

4. John Henry Cooke, *A Narrative of Events in the South of France and of the Attack on New Orleans in 1814 and 1815* (London: T. & W. Boone, 1835), 190–91.

5. Latour, *Historical Memoir of the War*, xlii–xliii.

6. Quoted in de Grummond, *Baratarians*, 93.

7. Bassett, *Correspondence of Andrew Jackson*, 2:127.

8. Latour, *Historical Memoir of the War*, 102–3.

9. Frank L. Owsley Jr., *Struggle for the Gulf Borderlands* (Tuscaloosa: University of Alabama Press, 2000), 146.

10. Vincent Nolte, *Fifty Years in Both Hemispheres* (New York: Redfield, 1854), 213.

11. Although the treaty was signed by the delegations, it still had to be ratified by the US Senate before taking effect.

12. De Grummond, *Baratarians*, 96–97.

13. Walker, Anderson, *The Life of Andrew Jackson* New York: Derby and Jackson, 1859), 211.

14. Cooke, *Narrative of Events*, 203.

15. De Grummond, *Baratarians*, 102–3.

16. Most of these bales belonged to Vincent Nolte. When Nolte complained, Livingston told him, "Well, Mr. Nolte, if this is your cotton, you at least will not think it any hardship to defend it." Nolte, *Fifty Years*, 215–16.

17. Robert Remini, *The Life of Andrew Jackson* (New York: Harper & Row, 1988), 98–99.

18. Alexander Walker, *Jackson and New Orleans: An Authentic Narrative of the Memorable Achievements of the American Army, Under Andrew Jackson, Before New Orleans, in the Winter of 1814, '15* (J. C. Derby, 1856), 257.

19. De Grummond, *Baratarians*, 106n25.

20. Bassett, *Correspondence of Andrew Jackson*, 2:130; De Grummond, *Baratarians*, 119.

21. Nolte, *Fifty Years*, 219.

CHAPTER 14: NEW ORLEANS: THE BATTLE OF
JANUARY 8, 1815

1. John Spencer Bassett, ed., *The Correspondence of Andrew Jackson*, 2 vols. (Washington, DC: Carnegie Institution of Washington, 1927), 2:132.

2. Alexander Walker, *Jackson and New Orleans: An Authentic Narrative of the Memorable Achievements of the American Army, Under Andrew Jackson, Before New Orleans, in the Winter of 1814, '15* (J. C. Derby, 1856), 318–19.

3. Jean Lucas de Grummond, *The Baratarians and the Battle of New Orleans* (Baton Rouge: LSU Press, 1961), 129–32.

4. Robert Remini, *Andrew Jackson: A Biography* (New York: Palgrave Macmillan, 2008), 111.

5. James Parton, *Life of Andrew Jackson*, vol. 2 (New York: Mason Brothers, 1860), 192.

6. Walker, *Jackson and New Orleans*, 326. Mullens would be court-martialed after the battle.

7. Quoted in Parton, *Life of Andrew Jackson*, 2:192.

8. John Henry Cooke, *A Narrative of Events in the South of France and of the Attack on New Orleans in 1814 and 1815* (London: T. & W. Boone, 1835), 229.

9. Ibid., 231.

10. Walker, *Jackson and New Orleans*, 327.

11. Anonymous, "A Contemporary Account of the Battle of New Orleans by a Soldier in the Ranks," *Louisiana Historical Quarterly* 9 (January 1926), 11.

12. Walker, *Jackson and New Orleans*, 329–31.

13. Cooke, *Narrative of Events*, 235.

14. Major A. Lacarrière Latour, *Historical Memoir of the War in West Florida and Louisiana* (Philadelphia: John Conrad, 1816), cli.

15. Quoted in Parton, *Life of Andrew Jackson*, 2:199.

16. Cooke, *Narrative of Events*, 256.

17. Parton, *Life of Andrew Jackson*, 2:200–201.

18. Walker, *Jackson and New Orleans*, 341; John Reid and John Henry Eaton, *The Life of Andrew Jackson* (Philadelphia: Carey & Son, 1817), 345; Latour, *Historical Memoir of the War*, lx–lxiv.

19. Parton, *Life of Andrew Jackson*, 2:208–9.

20. Quoted in ibid.

21. Walker, *Jackson and New Orleans*, 341–42.

22. "Contemporary Account," 14.

23. Bassett, *Correspondence of Andrew Jackson*, 2:143.

24. Latour, *Historical Memoir of the War*, clii–clvi.

25. Bassett, *Correspondence of Andrew Jackson*, 2:143.

26. Ibid., 2:133.

27. Ibid., 2:134.

28. Walker, *Jackson and New Orleans*, 361.

29. Vincent Nolte, *Fifty Years in Both Hemispheres* (New York: Redfield, 1854), 234.

30. Cooke, *Narrative of Events*, 273–74.

31. Parton, *Life of Andrew Jackson*, 2:267.

32. Quoted in ibid., 2:269–70. General Keane had eighteen hundred well-trained troops roughly nine miles from New Orleans. The American forces may have numbered four thousand but were scattered about, unsure where the British would land. Why didn't Keane continue into the city with his troops? He had the initiative, surprise, and numbers on his side. Had he done so, the

results would have been disastrous for Jackson. "The result of the affair of the 23d was the saving of Louisiana, chronicled Latour. Latour, *Historical Memoir of the War*, 112

CHAPTER 15: THE HERO OF NEW ORLEANS

1. John Spencer Bassett, ed., *The Correspondence of Andrew Jackson* 2 vols. (Washington, DC: Carnegie Institution of Washington, 1927), 2:150.

2. Ibid.

3. Major A. Lacarrière Latour, *Historical Memoir of the War in West Florida and Louisiana* (Philadelphia: John Conrad, 1816), clxxxii–clxxxvi.

4. Quoted in Robert Remini, *Andrew Jackson: A Biography* (New York: Palgrave Macmillan, 2008), 123.

5. Quoted in James Parton, *Life of Andrew Jackson*, vol. 2 (New York: Mason Brothers, 1860), 248.

6. Ibid., 2:253.

7. William Graham Sumner, *Andrew Jackson as a Public Man* (Boston: Houghton Mifflin, 1882), 51.

8. Even the treaty was disappointing. No mention was made of the orders in council or British impressment of American sailors—two major factors that caused the war.

9. Sumner, *Andrew Jackson*, 50.

10. Quoted in Parton, *Life of Andrew Jackson*, 2:257.

11. Bassett, *Correspondence of Andrew Jackson*, 2:148.

12. Ibid., 2:183.

13. Parton, *Life of Andrew Jackson*, 2:319.

14. Ibid., 2:329.

15. Ibid., 2:334.

16. Bassett, *Correspondence of Andrew Jackson*, 2:218.

CHAPTER 16: THE INDIAN QUESTION

1. John Spencer Bassett, ed., The *Correspondence of Andrew Jackson*, 2 vols. (Washington, DC: Carnegie Institution of Washington, 1927), 2:243.

2. Ibid., 2:77–78.

3. Ibid., 2:279–80.

4. Ibid., 2:280.

5. Jackson himself resorted to bribery when it suited him. See, for example, Robert Remini, *Jackson and the Course of American Empire, 1767–1821* (New York: Harper & Row, 1977), 328–30, for an example and discussion of this practice.

6. Andrew Jackson, *The Papers of Andrew Jackson*, vol. 2, ed. Harold D. Moser, Sharon Macpherson, and Charles F. Bryan Jr. (Knoxville: University of Tennessee Press, 1984), 226.

7. Quoted in Remini, *The Life of Andrew Jackson* (New York: Harper & Row, 1988), 113.

8. For a complete discussion of this complex subject see Remini's *Jackson and American Empire*, 321–40.

CHAPTER 17: THE FIRST SEMINOLE WAR

1. John Spencer Bassett, ed., *The Correspondence of Andrew Jackson*, 2 vols. (Washington, DC: Carnegie Institution of Washington, 1927), 2:241.

2. James Parton, *Life of Andrew Jackson* (New York: Mason Brothers, 1860), 406.

3. Harold D. Moser, David R. Hoth, and George H. Hoemann, eds., *The Papers of Andrew Jackson*, vol. 4, 1816–1820 (Knoxville: University of Tennessee Press, 1994), 107.

4. Ibid., 107. Arbuthnot was a seventy-year-old Scottish-born trader from the Bahamas. He came to Florida in 1817 to trade with the Indians and Spanish and took up their cause against the Americans, whom he believed were not living up to the Treaty of Ghent.

5. Bassett, *Correspondence of Andrew Jackson*, 2:306.

6. Parton, *Life of Andrew Jackson*, 2:429.

7. Ibid., 2:430. Parton provides ample proof of this assertion by quoting from a US Senate hearing in February 1819. The Second Seminole War, also known as the Florida War, was fought from 1835 to 1842.

8. Jackson, *Papers*, 4:153–54.

9. Parton, *Life of Andrew Jackson*, 2:430.

10. Bassett, *Correspondence of Andrew Jackson*, 2:340.

11. Ibid.

12. Ibid., 2:341–42.

13. Quoted in Robert Remini, *Andrew Jackson: A Biography* (New York: Palgrave Macmillan, 2008), 142.

14. Bassett, *Correspondence of Andrew Jackson*, 2:345–46.

15. Jackson, *Papers*, 4:165.

16. David S. Heidler and Jeanne T. Heidler, *Old Hickory's War* (Mechanicsburg, PA: Stackpole Books, 1996), 120. They also fault Monroe for not being more proactive in the situation. They conclude his management style was passivity. "Jackson lied about Monroe's authorization," they contend, "but Monroe had actually done worse. . . . He had done nothing" (121).

17. See the discussion of this discrepancy in Bassett, *Correspondence of Andrew Jackson*, 2: xi.

18. Ibid., 2:348.

19. Jackson, *Papers*, 4:170.

20. Ibid., 4:172.

21. Ibid., 4:184–85.

22. Heidler and Heidler, *Old Hickory's War*, 137.

23. Parton, *Life of Andrew Jackson*, 2:447–48.

24. Bassett, *Correspondence of Andrew Jackson*, 2:358–59.

25. Jackson, *Papers*, 4:186.

26. Ibid., 4:186–87.

27. Ibid., 4:199.

28. Quoted in Robert Remini, *The Life of Andrew Jackson* (New York: Harper & Row, 1988), 121.

29. A detailed account of the trial of these two is found in Remini, *Andrew Jackson: A Biography*, 155–59; and Heidler and Heidler, *Old Hickory's War*, 155–57; Jackson's own account of the events is found in Jackson, *Papers*, 4:197–200.

30. Bassett, *Correspondence of Andrew Jackson*, 2:360.

31. Jackson, *Papers*, 4:199.

32. Ibid., 4:200.

33. Ibid., 4:205–6.

34. Ibid.

35. Ibid., 4:209.

36. Ibid., 4:210.

37. Ibid., 4:211.

38. Ibid., 4:214–15.

39. Ibid., 4:213.

40. Parton, *Life of Andrew Jackson*, 2:485–87.

41. Remini, *Andrew Jackson: A Biography*, 170–172.

42. Due to Spanish foot dragging, it would not be until July 10, 1821, that the last troops would leave the territory and East and West Florida were united.

43. [[missing note]]

44. Heidler and Heidler, *Old Hickory's War*, 228, 231.

45. Parton, *Life of Andrew Jackson*, 2:566, 574-5; Remini, *Life of Andrew Jackson*, 127.

CHAPTER 18: JACKSON AS PRESIDENT

1. Andrew Jackson, *The Papers of Andrew Jackson*, vol. 5, Samuel B.

Smith and Harriet Chappell Owsley, eds.(Knoxville: University of Tennessee Press,) 29–30.

2. Ibid., 5:243.

3. For a detailed account of this election, see Robert Remini, *The Election of Andrew Jackson* (Philadelphia: Lippincott, 1963).

4. Robert Remini, *The Life of Andrew Jackson* (New York: Harper & Row, 1988), 164.

5. James Parton, *Life of Andrew Jackson*, vol. 3 (New York: Mason Brothers, 1860), 150–51; Jon Meacham, *American Lion: Andrew Jackson in the White House* (New York: Random House, 2008), 49; Remini, *Life of Andrew Jackson*, 168.

6. Parton, *Life of Andrew Jackson*, 3:153.

7. Ibid., 3:154.

8. Ibid., 3:156.

9. Ibid.

10. Quoted in Meacham, *American Lion*, 134.

11. Quoted in Remini, *Life of Andrew Jackson*, 239.

12. For a detailed discussion of this complex issue, see Meacham, *American Lion*, 226–31; Remini, *Life of Andrew Jackson*, 233–51.

13. Parton, *Life of Jackson*, 3:670.

14. Meacham, *America Lion*, 209–12; Remini, *Life of Andrew Jackson*, 261–77.

15. Remini, *Life of Andrew Jackson*, 274.

16. W. David Baird and Danney Goble, *The Story of Oklahoma* (Norman: University of Oklahoma Press, 1994), 133. The five civilized tribes include the Creeks, Chickasaws, Cherokees, Choctaws, and Seminoles.

17. Ibid., 133–34.

18. Ibid., 138

19. Remini, *Life of Andrew Jackson*, 218.

20. Quoted. in ibid., 216,

21. Ibid., 218. Baird and Goble, *Story of Oklahoma*, 133–46, contains a detailed account of the Indian removal.

22. Remini, *Life of Andrew Jackson*, 218–19.

CHAPTER 19: LEGACY

1. James Parton, *Life of Andrew Jackson*, vol. 3 (New York: Mason Brothers, 1860), 672.

2. Ibid., 641.

3. One need only to remember John F. Kennedy's Catholicism, Jimmy

Carter's "lust in his heart" interview, George W. Bush's flap over drug use, and Obama's supposed Muslim leanings, to name a few, to appreciate the quagmire he resolved to avoid.

4. Parton, *Life of Andrew Jackson,*, 3:647.

5. Ibid., 3:649.

6. Ibid. 3:679.

7. In 1831, the bullet he received from Thomas Hart Benton had worked its way down the arm and could be felt. It was giving the general discomfort so he ordered it removed. Without anesthesia, the doctor cut his arm, gave it a squeeze, and "out jumped the ball upon the floor." We do not know if he returned it to Benton. Remini, *Life of Andew Jackson*, 223, and Parton, *Life of Andrew Jackson*, 3:415.

8. Remini, *Life of Andrew Jackson*, 358.

9. Ibid., 395 n20.

10. Quoted in Meacham, *American Lion*, 345.

11. Parton, *Life of Andrew Jackson*, 2:485.

Bibliography

Annals of Congress. House of Representatives, 4th Congress, 2nd Session, p. 1737. http// memory.loc.gov/cgi-bin/ampage.

Anonymous. "A Contemporary Account of the Battle of New Orleans by a Soldier in the Ranks." *Louisiana Historical Quarterly* 9 (January 1926).

Baird, W. David, and Danney Goble. *The Story of Oklahoma.* Norman: University of Oklahoma Press, 1994.

Bassett, John Spencer, ed. *The Correspondence of Andrew Jackson.* 2 vols. Washington, DC: Carnegie Institution of Washington, 1927.

Blount, William. *Biographical Directory of the United States Congress.* http://bioguide. congress.gov/scripts/biodisplay.pl?index=b000570.

Booraem, Hendrik. *Young Hickory: The Making of Andrew Jackson.* Dallas: Taylor Publishing, 2001.

Brands, H. W. *Andrew Jackson: His Life and Times.* New York: Doubleday, 2005.

Buell, Augustus C. *A History of Andrew Jackson: Pioineer, Patriot, Soldier, Politician, President.* New York: Charles Scribner's, 1904.

Carter, Samuel, III. *Blaze of Glory.* New York: St. Martin's Press, 1971.

Cartwright, Peter. *Autobiography of Peter Cartwright: The Backwoods Preacher.* New York: Carlton & Porter, 1856.

Claiborne, J. F. H. *Mississippi as a Province, Territory and State.* 2 vols. Jackson, MS: Power & Barksdale, 1880.

Cooke, John Henry. *A Narrative of Events in the South of France and of the Attack on New Orleans in 1814 and 1815.* London: T. & W. Boone, 1835.

Crockett, Davy. *Narrative of the Life of Davy Crockett.* Baltimore: Carey & Hart Co., 1834.

De Grummond, Jane Lucas. *The Baratarians and the Battle of New Orleans.* Baton Rouge: Louisiana State University Press, 1961.

Gayarré, Charles. *History of Louisiana*. 4 vols. New York: Redfield & William J. Widdleton, 1854.

Halbert, Henry S., and Timothy H. Ball. *The Creek War of 1813 and 1814*. Tuscaloosa: University of Alabama Press, 1995.

Heidler, David S., and Jeanne T. Heidler. *Old Hickory's War*. Mechanicsburg, PA: Stackpole Books, 1996.

Heiskill, S. G. *Andrew Jackson and Early Tennessee History*. Nashville: Ambrose Printing, 1920.

Hunt, Louise Livingston. *Memoir of Mrs. Edward Livingston with Letters Hitherto Unpublished*. New York: Harper & Brothers, 1886.

James, Marquis. *The Life of Andrew Jackson, Complete in One Volume*. New York: Bobbs-Merrill, 1938.

Jennings, Paul. *A Colored Man's Reminiscences of James Madison*. Brooklyn: George C. Beadle, 1865. http://docsouth.unc.edu/neh/jennings/jennings.html.

Kendall, Amos. *Life of Andrew Jackson*. New York: Harper & Brothers, 1843.

Latour, Major A. Lacarrière. *Historical Memoir of the War in West Florida and Louisiana*. Philadelphia: John Conrad, 1816.

Lossing, Benson J. *The Pictorial Field-Book of the War of 1812*. Vol. 2. New York, 1868.

Meacham, Jon. *American Lion: Andrew Jackson in the White House*. New York: Random House, 2008.

Moser, Harold D., and J. Clint Clifft, eds. *The Papers of Andrew Jackson*. Vol. 6. Knoxville: University of Tennessee Press, 2002.

Moser, Harold D., David R. Hoth, and George H. Hoemann, eds. *The Papers of Andrew Jackson*. Vol. 4, 1816–1820. Knoxville: University of Tennessee Press, 1994.

Moser, Harold D., David R. Hoth, Sharon Macpherson, and John H. Reinbold, eds. *The Papers of Andrew Jackson*. Vol. 3, 1814-1815 Knoxville: University of Tennessee Press, 1991.

Moser, Harold D., Sharon Macpherson, and Charles F. Bryan, Jr., eds. *The Papers of Andrew Jackson*. Vol. 2, 1804–1813. Knoxville: University of Tennessee Press, 1984.

Nolte, Vincent. *Fifty Years in Both Hemispheres*. New York: Redfield, 1854.

Owsley, Frank L., Jr. *Struggle for the Gulf Borderlands*. Tuscaloosa: University of Alabama Press, 2

Parton, James. *Life of Andrew Jackson in Three Volumes*. New York: Mason Brothers, 1860.

Pickett, Albert J. *History of Alabama*. 2 vols. Charleston: Walker & James, 1851.

Putnam, Albigence. *History of Middle Tennessee* or, Life and Times of Gen. James Robertson. Nashville: A. W. Putnam, 1859.

Ramsey, J. G. M. *The Annals of Tennessee to the End of the Eighteenth Century*. Philadelphia: Lippincott & Co., 1853.

Reid, John, and John Henry Eaton. *The Life of Andrew Jackson*. Philadelphia: Carey & Son, 1817.

Reilly, Robin. *The British at the Gates*. New York: Putnam & Sons, 1974.

Remini, Robert V. *Andrew Jackson: A Biography*. New York: Palgrave Macmillan, 2008.

_____. *The Battle of New Orleans.* New York: Penguin Group, 1999.

_____. *The Life of Andrew Jackson.* New York: Harper & Row, 1988.

_____. *Andrew Jackson and the Course of American Empire, 1767–1821.* New York: Harper & Row, 1977.

_____. *The Election of Andrew Jackson.* Philadelphia: Lippincott, 1963.

Scheer, George, and Hugh Rankin. *Rebels and Redcoats.* Cleveland: World Publishing, 1957.

Shaw, Ronald E., ed. *Andrew Jackson, 1767–1845: Chronology, Documents, Bibliographical Aids.* Dobbs Ferry, NY: Oceana Publications, 1969.

Smith, Margaret Bayard. *The First Forty Years of Washington Society.* Ed. Gaillard Hunt. New York: Charles Scribner's Sons, 1906.

Smith, Sam B., and Harriet Chappell Owsley, eds. *The Papers of Andrew Jackson.* Vol. 1, 1770–1803. Knoxville: University of Tennessee Press, 1980.

Smith, Sam B., and Harriet Chappell Owsley, eds. *The Papers of Andrew Jackson.* Vol.5. *1825-1828.* Knoxville: University of Tennessee Press, 1980.

Sumner, William Graham. *Andrew Jackson as a Public Man.* Boston: Houghton Mifflin, 1882.

Walker, Alexander. *Jackson and New Orleans: An Authentic Narrative of the Memorable Achievements of the American Army, Under Andrew Jackson, Before New Orleans, in the Winter of 1814, '15.* New York: J. C. Derby, 1859.

Westminster Shorter Catechism, http://www. reformed.org/documents/WSC_frames. html.

THE | GENERALS ★

A series about leaders who stood out above the rest. Each general is known for his character and his drive to constantly strive for more. Of course each one has his flaws, but their ability to lead others and the loyalty shown by their soldiers establish these generals as historical figures worthy of recognition and study.

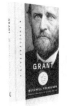

Grant:
Savior of the Union
By Mitchell Yockelson

Patton:
The Pursuit of Destiny
By Agostino von Hassell
and Ed Breslin

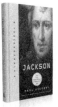

Jackson:
The Iron-Willed Commander
By Paul S. Vickery

Pershing:
Commander of the Great War
By John Perry

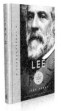

Lee:
A Life of Virtue
By John Perry

Sherman:
The Ruthless Victor
By Agostino von Hassell
and Ed Breslin

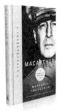

MacArthur:
America's General
By Mitchell Yockelson

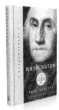

Washington:
A Legacy of Leadership
By Paul S. Vickery

For more information, visit www.TheGeneralsSeries.com
Available wherever books and ebooks are sold.